Becoming an Ex-Diabetic
Use your mind to prevent, manage or even reverse Type 2 diabetes

Becoming an
Ex-diabetic

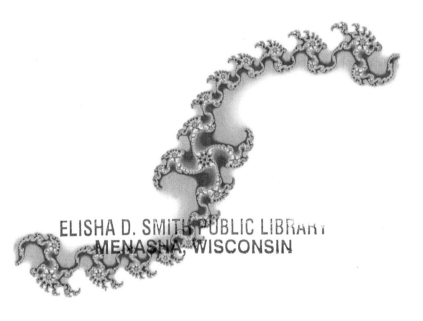

Use your mind to prevent, manage
or even **reverse** Type 2 diabetes

BARRY LANDSBERG

Anoma PRESS

Becoming an Ex-Diabetic
Use your mind to prevent, manage or even *reverse* Type 2 diabetes

First published in 2013 by
Anoma Press Ltd
48 St Vincent Drive, St Albans, Herts, AL1 5SJ UK
info@anomapress.com
www.anomapress.com

Cover design by Michael Inns
Artwork by Karen Gladwell

Printed on acid-free paper from managed forests.
This book is printed on demand to fulfill orders,
so no copies will be remaindered or pulped.

ISBN 978-1-908746-78-8

Contents

Prologue

It had been a very hot week, and I was on a business trip working with a customer in Belgium. This was a great excuse to eat and drink to my total satisfaction, which usually meant not stopping until I couldn't eat any more. Indeed, I was still smug from having charmed a whole pot of pâté de foie gras from a Channel Tunnel attendant, and happily eaten it all while waiting to get to the French side of the Channel.

I was staying in the ground-floor wing of a hotel, where the August sun mercilessly heated the room, and I had suffered three very hot nights. As we had worked long and hard during the day, I deserved to share a bottle of wine with my colleague. To my satisfaction, my colleague was not a big eater or drinker, so each night I had the lion's share of the bottle.

It was time to drive back to England and, as always, I planned to stop at the cheap supermarkets in Calais, to fill up my car with as much cheese, wine and beer as I could. Before I reached Calais, I developed a strong pain in the lower part of my stomach and started feeling increasingly sick and dizzy. Somehow, I got to the supermarket, and still highly motivated to buy food and drink, staggered round the store, tried to pick up a few bottles and didn't have the energy to even lift them. Then I saw a counter where free samples of wine were being given. With as much humour as I could muster, I went up and said, "I can't believe I am asking this. You are giving free wine, but all I want is a glass of water. I am not feeling very well." The man behind the counter immediately called for an ambulance and, despite my protests, they gave me oxygen and carried me off to the nearest hospital.

Once in the hospital, they put me on a saline drip and told me I was severely dehydrated. However, they took some blood samples, and the next day they refused me a chocolate drink with my breakfast, saying, "vous êtes diabétique." I didn't even know exactly what diabetic meant, and they kept adding insulin to my saline drip, taking blood samples for blood sugar measurements every few hours, even during the night, and telling me I was too ill to drive back home. It took me three days to break out of the hospital, including having to arrange for a driver to come over to Calais and drive me home. Despite how good I was feeling, they insisted that I check into a hospital as soon as I got back to England.

I didn't know it at the time, but that was the start of a bigger journey, and a transformation, that affected every part of my life.

Introduction

If you are reading this book, you probably have some kind of concern about blood sugar levels – whether for yourself or on behalf of someone you care about. That concern might be for the future, or already showing up as diabetic symptoms or from blood sugar measurements.

The main aim of this book is to present ideas and new ways of thinking that can help you deal successfully with these concerns in a healthy way, and maintain this in the longer term as easily and naturally as possible.

Why am I writing this book?

I entered the 21st century as someone who was very overweight, loved food and hated exercise. At that time, I was almost 50 years old, and did not take care of my health in any way. As a direct result, I developed Type 2 diabetes. My blood sugar is now at a very healthy level without the use of medication, and as a result I have been removed from the diabetic register.

I know what it's like to be very overweight and start puffing after walking only a few hundred yards. I know what it's like to be so obsessed with eating food that the very idea of losing weight seems impossibly daunting. I also know what it's like to be told that you have Type 2 diabetes.

Now I am almost 40 kilograms lighter, have overcome and reversed the diabetes, and maintained this for over ten years. Not by iron will and strict discipline, and not by following a particular diet regime. The most important thing was to start thinking differently, and then it all became easier to achieve the result and, more importantly, to maintain in the long term while still living a normal life. Along the way, I collected together and adopted ways of thinking that support the achievement and maintenance of a lifestyle that can prevent, control or even reverse Type 2 diabetes.

When I look at what is happening in the world with respect to the rapid increase of obesity and diabetes, it is clear that anything we can do to help stem this increase and help people prevent or reverse diabetes is extremely worthwhile. I am writing this book to share these ideas in the hope that this will inspire people to action and help make a difference in their lives.

CHAPTER ONE

Modern-day trends and obesity

Type 2 diabetes is a condition leading to a level of sugar in the blood that is too high, because the body cannot process and use the sugar properly. This has a large number of serious health consequences. The theme of this book is to describe lifestyle changes to prevent, manage or even reverse Type 2 diabetes, and present some mental tools and strategies to help make and maintain those lifestyle changes. There are many contributing factors to Type 2 diabetes, including genetics, ethnicity, gender and age. However, as Type 2 diabetes is increasing steadily in most countries worldwide, lifestyle is clearly a major factor in a large majority of these cases.

There is a very strong link between Type 2 diabetes and obesity. So this first chapter will focus only on obesity and the challenge that modern-day lifestyle presents. It starts with my personal experience and thoughts of being forever stuck with being overweight.

My journey

A lot of what happened to me as a child I see happening around me today. As many parents do, I was encouraged to eat everything that was on my plate, and reinforced as being a good boy if I finished it all.

Cakes and sweets were often given as a reward, and withdrawn as a punishment. Treats like birthday parties always involved eating lots of sweet food. So it is no wonder that the taste of sweet food starts to become associated with comfort and reward.

For breakfast, we had sugar-coated cereals, and we were bought sweets on a weekly basis.

During my early teens, I was at a school that used to give out exercise as a punishment. If we were seen to misbehave, we had to run a number of times round the tennis courts, and the worse the crime, the more rounds we had to do. Any serious misdemeanours were met with a cross-country run. If I can make an appeal so early in the book, it would be for schools to think very carefully about giving out any kind of treatment that could make children think of exercise as a punishment. From then on, I became an exercise hater, dreading the physical education lessons in later schools.

It was also during my early teens that I heard to my shock the comment from a fellow pupil, "Barry, you are joining the fat community." Yes – I was starting to put on weight.

As a young adult, I became very focused on food. I remember feeling proud of how much I could eat. Once, on a business trip, the chef said to me with astonishment, "Barry, I have seen a plate piled high with chicken, but never before seen a plate piled high with bones." At the time, I was very amused and took it as a compliment to my eating prowess, of which I was very proud.

It is one thing not to want to leave food on the plate. As I got older, I remember the feeling of discomfort when *other people* left food on their plates. I used to plan a strategy on how to get it without being seen, and was so driven and obsessive that I was often successful.

I also remember going on business trips, and driving to the airport as fast as I could with one thought on my mind – to arrive in time to be able to buy and eat a huge double cheeseburger and chips before the flight took off. I felt good when I felt full, sometimes so full I could not move, and when I was not full I called it being hungry.

What do many people do when they feel they are overweight? They go on a diet. I tried various diets and even improvised some of my own, all based on restricting food and being hungry. However, every time I lost any weight, somehow the diet fizzled out, and I was back where I started.

By the time I was in my late forties, I had fully accepted my large size and my lifestyle. Indeed, I used to enjoy doing a Pavarotti skit on stage at the village Christmas party, making jokes about my size. I also made a great Santa Claus.

I was very focused on eating, and always thinking about the next meal, or opportunity to eat. If I was away working, it did not matter whether I was hungry or not. I would order large plates of food because I *deserved* it after a long and hard day's work. I remember laughing when a colleague suggested having only a light meal.

In addition, I was an exercise hater, and avoided exercise in any form. Once, outside a fitness centre in a hotel, I said to a colleague with a laugh, "Look at these people who pay money to exercise. I would pay money *not* to exercise."

My level of physical fitness was such that when I would walk the dogs with my wife, I would stop and point out different things of interest, only to allow me to stop for a bit and hide the fact I was actually out of breath.

As I got even bigger, there was a part of me that did not recognise my increasing size. I started walking into doors, and appeared to become increasingly clumsy as I was misjudging the space needed to move from one place to another. This led to me becoming the butt of quite a few less than gentle jokes made at my expense.

The most embarrassing thing that happened to me was a visit to a fully automated newspaper printing plant. I was alone in the room where the presses were, and saw an interesting machine. It had a lot of dials and a big red emergency button. I was interested and leaned forward to look at the dials more closely, and to my horror my stomach pushed against the emergency button and stopped the press. I ran and hid in a corner of the room while a crowd of people came to the console, discussing furiously what might have happened.

One final note to this part of the story. Many of us have well-meaning friends or relatives who, with the best of intentions, try to help by giving advice, or telling you to slim down, or even not eat that delicacy that you already have in your hands. I remember occasions when that happened, and I dug my heels in. It didn't matter how true or good the advice was, the more it came, the more I resisted.

So, when I reached 50, my large size was a permanent part of my personality. I felt I was the last person on earth who could possibly lose weight, let alone become fit. Every time I had tried, it had led to total failure. There seemed no way out of it. I was not prepared to starve myself, or jump into doing stupid exercises – anyway these were a punishment for me. It was surely too late for me now I had passed 50.

So I had totally given up. I could not see anything that could change it. And this is how I would be for the rest of my life.

Modern-day environment

We are living in a society where, in general, people are eating larger quantities of food, eating less nutritious food, and doing less physical activity than was the case one or two generations ago. This is having a very serious effect on our health.

The average weight of the population is increasing, and with it come a host of health issues. These include high blood pressure, strokes, heart disease, joint problems, liver disease, and have even been linked to cancer. The next chapter focuses on diabetes and less on these other issues, even though each one is crucial in its own right. Along with Type 2 diabetes, the personal cost as well as the financial cost of dealing with these health issues is enormous.

So, where does this all come from? Are we all suddenly deciding to behave differently from our ancestors? I will suggest that many of us are simply caught up in the modern-day environment, which is full of traps for the unwary. Ways to navigate these will be described later in the book.

We are under attack

The combination of the food industry and fast food takeaway outlets is totally changing the way we eat within one or two generations.

We are encouraged to eat highly processed foods which are packed with unhealthy fat, salt and sugar. There is intense advertising for burgers, fried food, sweet drinks and unhealthily sweetened breakfast cereals.

There is a lot of research sponsored by the food industry to find additives that override the satiety signals in your body that tell you 'I have eaten enough', and even try to get you addicted to eating their food. They have studied the optimum ratios of added sugar, salt and fat to derive the greatest pleasure from eating. The use of appetite-inducing additives in large quantities, such as monosodium glutamate (MSG) and many other similar additives, is widespread. Indeed, one food manufacturer proudly advertises that once you eat some of their food, you can't stop. Unfortunately they really mean it, as they have put additives in to help ensure this becomes as true as possible.

There are also many other traps. With clever advertising, manufacturers try to make you believe that eating their food is healthy. While in a few cases this may be true, more often healthy low-fat options contain extra salt and sugar, and similarly foods claiming to be healthy due to reduced sugar may contain extra fat. It is very easy to fall into these traps.

Next are the fast food outlets. In this modern age, we are all very busy and don't find it easy to make the time to eat healthy food. Most fast food is based on refined flour, sugar, and the worst kind of fats. The fibre and nutrients have in most cases been totally removed. These outlets are generally cheaper than healthier food, and available from early morning until very late at night. They fit very nicely into busy lifestyles, where a fast and convenient meal is the easiest option. They also provide instant satisfaction, which is another ingredient of modern-day lifestyle. Such food is now available in an increasing number of places – petrol stations, coffee bars, 24-hour supermarkets, and bus and train stations. And the more such food is constantly available and visible, the more tempting it is to eat it.

There is also a trend to offer increasingly larger portions. This could be through 'eat all you can for a fixed price' buffet-style restaurants, or simply to offer larger single portions. For example, a standard beefburger is now double the size, and sugared fizzy soft drinks five times larger than they were in the 1960s.

All of these are over and above the traditional social, family and cultural pressures on us to eat and drink. Almost every celebration – whether a reunion, party, wedding, or special or religious non-fasting occasion – is centred on eating together.

Even as adults, going out for a meal is often a reward for good behaviour or achievement. It is hard to imagine a celebration which features sparkling water and salad.

For those who like to go out for a drink in a group, there is a 'rounds' system where each person in turn buys the group a drink. This can be hard to duck out of.

Putting all of this together, we are under attack in many ways. The net result is that, as a society, we are on average eating more calories than previous generations, and in general less healthy foods.

We are less active

Another modern-day trend is that we tend to do less activity on a daily basis than in previous generations.

There is an increasing trend for jobs to be done sitting all day at a computer and, in some cases, sitting at home without even travelling from one place to another.

Modern entertainment is often at a computer or video game station, and televisions and video/DVD players have remote controls so one can sit still watching for hours. Mobile phones can simply be pulled out of a pocket and used without having to go anywhere.

There is also online shopping where we don't even have to go out to a store, and when we do, there are usually lifts or escalators to make sure we don't have to exert ourselves. Some airports have a travelling conveyor belt to minimise the walking distance. With the continuing increase of labour-saving devices, which admittedly do enable us to get more done in less time, the net result is that we move less. This means we burn up less energy, and also allow our muscles to become underused.

Perhaps the worst of both worlds is the drive-through fast food outlet, where one can simply sit in the car without moving, and buy and eat highly processed fattening food.

How the body reacts

Imagine what life might have been like many thousands of years ago, and what kind of evolutionary changes were needed to keep us alive under the conditions that we as a species would have been facing.

It is likely that food was scarce, and there would be periods when there was no food at all. Also, it would have been necessary to be active in many ways, whether hunting, escaping from predators, or collecting or preparing food. The kind of food available would have been meat, fish and plant-based foods, all of which release sugar into the bloodstream slowly.

To handle such periods of scarcity, the body has developed quite a few clever mechanisms to ensure the maximum chance of survival. It signals intense hunger, especially for fats and sugars. It would also ramp up the fat-storing part of the metabolism in order to store whatever meagre supplies of food became available. It would start breaking down muscle tissue for energy instead of fat in order to conserve vital energy for as long as possible.

Without these strategies, we might not have survived as a species. As evolutionary processes are slow, in the 5,000-10,000 years since then, our bodies still react in the same way. For this reason, while we are built to survive scarcity, we are totally defenceless against the combination of overfeeding and low activity – especially with a diet of highly processed high-fat and sugary food. This results in a population that, on average, is increasing in weight at an alarming rate. It also stresses the body's ability to control blood sugar, and results in a similar increase in Type 2 diabetes.

However, we do have one evolutionary advantage, and that is a powerful brain. This may end up as being our sole defence against what in evolutionary terms is a potentially lethal threat to our health.

Obesity trends

The Organisation for Economic Co-operation and Development (OECD) is an international organisation which has produced a comprehensive worldwide report on obesity*. To outline the numbers and trends, their results for the United States and the United Kingdom are presented below. However, these trends are reflected worldwide. Even some of the countries who did not have many overweight people in their population are beginning to show an increase, and the speed of the increase appears to be related to the incidence of fast food outlets springing up.

Their statistics show that for the United Kingdom, 57% of the adult population are defined as overweight, of which 24% are classed as obese.

For the United States, 64% of the adult population are defined as overweight, of which 38% are classed as obese.

We will define more precisely what these categories are in a later chapter. For now, it is fair to say that most people in the overweight category are at medium- or long-term risk of eventually becoming diabetic, while those in the obese category stand to face many health issues, including a high risk of becoming diabetic. The risk does seem to depend on a lot of different factors, including genetics, ethnicity, gender and age. However, whatever the natural tendency may be, the risk is increased for everyone in these weight categories. This is over half the adult population for the UK, the USA and indeed many other countries too.

The numbers seem even more worrying when looking at the trends. The percentage in the obese category has increased by 50% for the UK and the USA over 20 years, and in some countries such as Australia and New Zealand, it has more than doubled.

The UK currently has the same level of obesity that the USA had 20 years ago. The trend in both countries is still reported to be increasing year by year, and it is not hard to imagine that the UK will match the USA statistics within 20 years. Other countries worldwide are following a similar trend.

In conclusion, we are facing an increasingly hostile environment for our health. It is like swimming upstream to keep the population as a whole healthy, and the figures and trends are showing this clearly.

This book provides some tools, using our evolutionary advantage of a powerful brain, to help reduce the strength of the current, and make the journey easier to navigate.

---

* Based on data from pages 54 and 55 from OECD (2011), Health at a Glance 2011: OECD Indicators, OECD Publishing

CHAPTER TWO

Diabetes

There is a dramatic worldwide increase in Type 2 diabetes. This chapter explains in simple terms the background behind the different kinds of diabetes and why it is so important to build in a lifestyle to prevent it happening in the first place, or managing and in some cases even reversing it if it is already diagnosed. It also describes what happens in terms of insulin when we eat a meal. This gives a good foundation for understanding some of the most effective actions to tackle diabetes.

My journey

Throughout my forties, I was getting increasingly overweight. With only one exception, I had done absolutely nothing about it. About ten years earlier, I was taking sugar in every cup of coffee, and the thought came to me, long before I even understood what diabetes was, that it might be bad for me. So I decided to cut it out and stop taking sugar in my drinks. That was the only concession I made towards my health.

I remember on a visit to the doctor's surgery, one of the doctors rudely and abruptly asked me if I was pregnant. It was a missed opportunity, as I was not offered any kind of blood test to check out my sugar levels. These tests are fast, inexpensive and immediate, and could help make a bigger impact on the prevention of Type 2 diabetes.

As I turned 50, something new started to happen. I kept having to get up to go to the toilet, and this increased to up to five or six times a night. At that time, I simply thought that now I was 50 I was getting old and my bladder was simply getting weaker.

About the same time, I also started getting an intense thirst for water. I had hardly ever drunk water in my life, always preferring fizzy soft drinks. But suddenly, I was gulping down very large quantities of water.

At this point, I knew so little about diabetes that I did not recognise these as classic symptoms of the disease. So I continued with my current lifestyle. Something had to give, and in the end it did!

It was a very hot August, and I was working in Belgium and staying in a hotel where the rooms were like ovens. When I drove back to Calais to get the ferry home, I started feeling very sick indeed, and was so unable to even stand up properly that someone called the paramedics to give me oxygen and take me to hospital. As it turned out, the reason for my collapse was self-inflicted dehydration, and it was only through routine tests that they discovered a very high level of sugar in my blood. They added insulin to my saline drip and insisted I was very ill. After three days in the hospital, I got back home. My initial reaction was that I was broken, and simply wanted 'them' to fix it for me.

I had an argument with my doctor the very next day, who said he would give me three months before he did anything. If I could get my blood sugar levels down to 13 mmol/l (240 mg/dl) within three months, he would then decide what medication to put me on and give me a prescription. The significance of these numbers will be described later in this chapter. In the meantime, he said I should diet and also do exercise. I was very angry with him for not helping me in the way I thought I needed it, and probably not at my most pleasant.

However, it helped me make a crucial transition. I was not a victim of bad luck. This was something I had inflicted, albeit unknowingly, on myself. My doctor had been right! It was now time to accept full responsibility and see to what extent I could make a difference. For this, I am eternally grateful to my doctor for having had the courage to stand up to me.

Then began a long and very worthwhile project towards a healthy lifestyle, and a whole new area of knowledge.

How do we control blood sugar?

It is crucial to our survival to control tightly the amount of sugar that is in our blood. Too much, and we suffer long-term severe complications. Too little, and one can go into a coma. Both extremes are lethal. So the body has a complex set of processes to keep the blood sugar at the right level.

As a comparison, it does a similar thing with temperature. Too warm, and it acts to cool you down by producing sweat, and dilating blood vessels so that heat escapes thought the skin. Too cold, and it acts to warm you up by shivering, and narrowing blood vessels to keep the heat inside the body.

The body does something similar with blood sugar. We have an organ called the pancreas, which is located just below and behind the stomach. The pancreas has many different and important functions, and one of them is to produce a hormone called insulin.

The insulin reduces the blood sugar in three major ways. Firstly, it enables the sugar to be stored in our muscles, so that it can be used directly for movement and activity. Secondly, it enables the sugar to be stored in the liver, so that the body can use it for more extended periods of activity. Thirdly, it triggers the intake of sugar into the fat cells all over your body, to be converted to fat and stored. Insulin can be regarded as a fat storage hormone.

As always in the body, there is an opposite process to increase the blood sugar level when it gets low, via a hormone called glucagon, which also comes from the pancreas. So, insulin and glucagon work together to keep the blood sugar level at the correct value.

Anatomy of a meal

In order to appreciate some of the ideas in this book, let us outline what happens when a healthy person eats a meal.

As the meal is digested, sugar is released into the bloodstream in the form of glucose. This triggers the pancreas to release insulin into the blood. The higher the amount of sugar, or the faster it enters the bloodstream, the more insulin is released.

At this point, insulin and other hormones are called in to signal that enough has been eaten. We call this satiety, and these hormones switch off the sense of hunger and also reduce how enjoyable the taste of the food is. This process takes about 20 minutes.

With a healthy meal, such as our early ancestors would have eaten, the blood sugar rises slowly and continues over maybe a few hours. The amount of insulin released is relatively low, the sugar is stored in the liver and muscles and the remainder is converted to fat and stored. As the blood sugar goes down, the level of insulin also falls. Note that both the glucose and the insulin can take a few hours to get back to the pre-meal level. This means the energy is available over a long period of time, and there is unlikely to be any physical sensation of hunger.

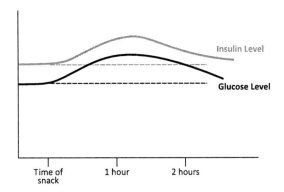

Consider another type of meal consisting of food that releases a very large burst of sugar into the bloodstream in a very short time. This happens very often with modern-day highly processed foods, for example a Danish pastry covered with icing, a croissant with honey, or simply a large sugared fizzy drink.

In this case, there is a large burst of insulin, and over the two hours it takes for the insulin to get back to the pre-meal level, it removes a lot of the sugar from the blood, to the point that one to two hours afterwards the blood sugar level is significantly lower. Here is an idea of what is taking place:

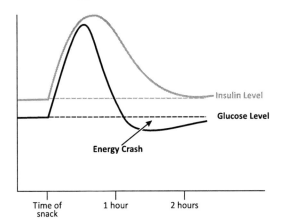

One of the results is that it becomes more difficult to concentrate, as the brain requires a constant amount of glucose to function properly. This could lead to fuzzy thinking, restlessness or irritability. Equally significantly, a lower blood sugar level results in lower energy being available, and also triggers the hunger sensation.

So a vicious circle is set up. Within one to two hours of eating such a meal or snack, there is an energy crash and often a strong feeling of hunger, which often triggers an urge for a repeat snack. This can cycle many times a day.

Now, take one more scenario, which is typical of someone with Type 2 diabetes, or even in the undiagnosed early stages, which we call prediabetes. Imagine that the same high-sugar snack is consumed by someone whose ability to use their insulin fully is impaired. When this happens, the muscles and the liver do not readily take in the sugar. However, the fat cells can *always* use the insulin to store the sugar, so it naturally gets converted to fat. The levels of insulin and sugar remain in the blood for a much longer time, and there is no energy crash. The sugar spike now broadens to a much wider peak as it stays in the blood for a longer time, and is mainly converted into fat and stored. This occurs more readily than for a person without Type 2 diabetes. Also, the triggers that signal satisfaction tend to be decreased, further fuelling high sugar eating.

What is diabetes?

So, what exactly is diabetes? There are many different kinds of diabetes which at first sight look very different and complicated. However, all of the different kinds are based on one or both of the following issues:

▶ The inability of the pancreas to produce insulin. This can be partial, or total.

▶ The inability of the body to use the insulin that is produced correctly. This will be referred to often in this book, and is called insulin resistance.

Diabetes shows itself by an increase in blood sugar level. So let us now define the levels.

The units used in the United Kingdom are called mmol/l (millimoles per litre). In the United States, the units used are the number of milligrams in one decilitre (100 cc) of blood. The conversion factor is 1 mmol/l = 18 mg/dl, and 100 mg/dl = 5.6 mmol/l. So, multiply mmol/l by 18 to get mg/dl, and divide mg/dl by 18 to get mmol/l.

A healthy person would typically have, before breakfast, a blood sugar level of between about 4 mmol/l (72 mg/dl) and 6 mmol/l (108 mg/dl).

For completeness, there is also a European standard, expressed in grams/litre, and these numbers are simply 100 times smaller than the United States standard.

There are ways of defining whether a person is on the way to becoming diabetic, but has not yet progressed enough to be diagnosed as such. One of them is called prediabetes, and this can almost always be halted by lifestyle changes. So it is a good idea to start acting on the ideas described later in this book if prediabetes is suspected or discovered, in order to prevent more serious problems at a later date.

Here are the definitions, in terms of blood sugar values, used to decide an initial diagnosis of diabetes or prediabetes:

	Fasting sugar level	After glucose test
Healthy	*Below 6.1 mmol/l*	Below 7.8 mmol/l
	Below 110 mg/dl	Below 140 mg/dl
Prediabetic	*6.1 – 7.0 mmol/l*	7.8 – 11.1 mmol/l
	110 – 125 mg/dl	140 – 200 mg/dl
Diabetic	*Above 7.0 mmol/l*	Above 11.1 mmol/l
	Above 136 mg/dl	Above 200 mg/dl

The glucose tolerance test in the table above measures how quickly glucose is taken out of the bloodstream. After the fasting blood sugar level is taken, a dose of 75g of glucose solution is drunk, and the blood sugar level measured two hours afterwards.

Apart from prediabetes, there is another popular indicator of risk, called metabolic syndrome. This is a cluster of health factors, one of which is blood pressure lower than 130/85 mm Hg, and it also takes into account cholesterol and fat levels in blood, waist size as well as blood sugar measurements. It is a good general health indicator, especially for heart disease, and is worth knowing about. It is also interesting to note that metabolic syndrome defines a fasting blood glucose level of greater than 5.6 mmol/l (100 mg/dl) as an indicator of potential health risk. This is more stringent than the values in the above table, and it might be wise to regard this value as a trigger for preventative action to reduce insulin resistance. Although the focus of this book is dealing with Type 2 diabetes, reducing weight and blood sugar levels is also likely to have a very positive effect on all the other metabolic syndrome criteria, with all its corresponding health benefits. For these reasons, prediabetes will be referred to as the main warning sign in the context of Type 2 diabetes.

Finally, there is another very useful indicator which shows the average sugar level over two to three months. It is called HbA1c, and is popularly referred to as A1c. It is basically the amount of glucose that sticks to the blood molecules. In the past it has only been used as a guideline, but in some countries it is being used increasingly for initial diagnosis of diabetes, either in isolation or in conjunction with the blood sugar level tests described above.

In the context of diagnosis, HbA1c levels below 5.7% (39 mmol/mol) can be considered healthy, up to 6.4% (46 mmol/mol) as a prediabetic indicator, and above 6.5% (48 mmol/mol) as an indicator of diabetes. Many people with diabetes, especially those with Type 1 diabetes, use A1c measurements as a useful guideline to gauge how well they have been controlling their average blood sugar levels.

Causes and types of diabetes

There are various varieties of diabetes, and now is a good time to mention that the word diabetes is often referred to as 'diabetes mellitus', which covers all forms of diabetes where the blood sugar rises. There is another form called 'diabetes insipidus', which is a kidney illness and has nothing to do with blood sugar levels, but shows very similar initial symptoms. For the rest of this book, the word diabetes will be taken to mean diabetes mellitus.

Here are some of the different varieties:

Type 1 diabetes

This is where the immune system in the body has actually attacked the cells of the pancreas and destroyed them. This gives rise to an inability to produce insulin.

Modern surgical transplant of pancreas or insulin-producing cells can hold out hope of a reprieve or cure, but there is no known lifestyle change that would influence the onset or the reversal of Type 1 diabetes. In this case, one is dependent on taking insulin in order to survive. With careful management of insulin intake against carbohydrate input and energy expenditure, there is no reason why Type 1 diabetes should put any limits on what people can achieve, and there are many professional athletes and long-distance runners with Type 1 diabetes.

Type 2 diabetes

This is where there is an inability to use correctly the insulin that is produced, and is called insulin resistance. This gives rise to increased levels of sugar in the blood, and also increased levels of insulin. Type 2 diabetes is somewhat insidious in that there are no pronounced symptoms until the blood sugar reaches a high level. So without testing, it is almost impossible to know whether you are prediabetic, or whether your blood sugar is higher than the threshold. It is only when it has already progressed a long way that the symptoms start to show. Typically, the initial symptoms are a constant thirst, excessive urination, tiredness and in some cases an inexplicable loss of weight. With time, the pancreas may deteriorate under the stress of having to produce a higher level of insulin than it is designed to do. This can eventually lead to the need to become insulin dependent.

This is the form of diabetes that is the main topic of this book, and in many cases the onset is dependent on lifestyle, as is also its management and reversal.

A couple of generations ago, Type 1 diabetes was called 'juvenile onset diabetes' as it was mainly the younger people who contracted it, and Type 2 diabetes was called 'adult onset diabetes' as it was generally the older adults who contracted it. However, under the increasing influence of modern lifestyles, teenagers and even younger children are now also starting to develop Type 2 diabetes, and these terms are being dropped.

Gestational diabetes

Insulin resistance is a complex process, and is affected by other hormones in the body. The female hormone oestrogen tends to reduce insulin resistance, while the hormone progesterone tends to increase it. Indeed, there are some people whose blood sugar can naturally go dangerously low during the oestrogen-rich part of the monthly cycle.

The middle and later parts of a pregnancy are times of very high levels of progesterone. It is also a time of increased cortisol production, which in other contexts acts as a stress hormone, and this also raises insulin resistance. These can push the insulin resistance high enough to cross the diabetic threshold. Gestational diabetes is the occurrence of Type 2 diabetes during pregnancy in women who did not have it before pregnancy, and can often result in the birth of larger babies. In most cases, it is a temporary condition of heightened insulin resistance, and blood sugar returns to normal afterwards. However, many women who have had gestational diabetes go on to develop full Type 2 diabetes later in life, and it is an appropriate trigger for deciding to take the kind of actions described in this book.

LADA

This stands for Latent Autoimmune Diabetes of Adulthood. It has sometimes been referred to as Type 1.5 diabetes. It is essentially where the insulin-producing cells in the pancreas deteriorate slowly, and in that sense is a variant of Type 1 diabetes. However, to all outward appearances it can, in many cases, look like Type 2 diabetes at first, even to doctors.

One problem is that the usual treatment for Type 2 diabetes is to give medication that counters insulin resistance, and that is not what LADA patients are suffering from.

If it is progressive, then despite medication and even the strategies outlined in this book, the end result is likely to be insulin dependence.

MODY

This stands for Maturity Onset of Diabetes for the Young, and is also sometimes referred to as monogenic diabetes as it is usually due to the mutation of one gene. Confusingly, it is also sometimes referred to as Type 1.5 diabetes. MODY is in itself a collection of different types of diabetes, each one apparently related to a different genetic issue. Some forms of MODY can develop into full Type 1 diabetes, even at the age of 50, and some forms can even recover insulin production with certain drugs. All forms of MODY show up as an ineffective production of insulin by the pancreas.

Double diabetes

This is usually a progression of Type 1 diabetes, where in addition to the pancreas not producing insulin, the body is highly insulin resistant. This is not a good combination at all. In many cases the onset of insulin resistance can be related to lifestyle.

Prediabetes

Prediabetes is simply a condition where the first phase of progression towards contracting Type 2 diabetes has already started. It is characterised by some insulin resistance, and a slightly raised blood sugar level. There are a large number of people with this condition, most of whom are totally unaware of this.

Summary of diabetes types

If you have been recently diagnosed as Type 2 diabetic or prediabetic, especially if you are younger than middle age and not overweight, it is worth being aware of all of these, especially if lifestyle changes and medication for insulin resistance (such as Metformin) have little effect in reducing the blood sugar levels. Not every doctor knows about all of these, and it may be worth asking for a LADA or MODY check. These are not given automatically, as they are more expensive and account for a minority of the diabetic population.

The main theme of this book is Type 2 diabetes, which accounts for over 90% of the adult diabetic population. However, each category of diabetes will benefit from ensuring insulin resistance is held as low as possible, and I would hope that the ideas in this book will be useful no matter what type of diabetes you might be facing.

There are many factors that affect the risk of Type 2 diabetes. Some factors that are fixed and cannot be influenced are genetic factors, which cover family incidence and also ethnic background. Similarly, gender and age influence the likelihood of contracting it too. It is clear that some people are simply more likely to contract it than others.

Having said that, there are some modifiable factors too, which are under your control. These are factors that in principle you *can* do something about, as they depend on your lifestyle.

A major factor for Type 2 diabetes is being overweight. Fats in the bloodstream increase insulin resistance in muscles, and also a fatty liver will become less sensitive to insulin. While obesity is strongly linked to Type 2 diabetes, note that a high level of insulin increases fat storage, and also inhibits the ability to burn the fat for energy. Insulin resistance therefore fuels the process of becoming increasingly overweight. Obesity and insulin resistance work together in a vicious circle.

Another factor is whether the blood is loaded with spikes of sugar. Eating foods that release sugar into the blood slowly will help prevent Type 2 diabetes, and habitual consumption of fast-release sugar foods will increase the risk significantly.

It has also been found that smoking increases insulin resistance and raises blood sugar levels.

Yet another important lifestyle factor is physical activity. A sedentary lifestyle encourages insulin resistance, which can start the whole cycle. Regular physical activity reduces insulin resistance by priming the muscles to accept insulin as a signal to take in sugar from the blood. Exercise is an important part of adopting a lifestyle that maintains a lower level of sugar and insulin in the blood.

Finally, it is interesting to quantify just how much sugar is actually contained in the blood. We have around five litres of blood, and with a healthy fasting sugar level of about 100 mg/dl (or one gram/ litre), this is a total of about five grams, or just one teaspoonful of sugar. It can of course be slightly higher, for instance after meals. So this means that for a healthy person the blood only contains between one and two teaspoons of sugar at any time.

Long-term effects

Type 2 diabetes is characterised by a raised level of blood sugar and insulin. This is toxic and has a large number of devastating long-term effects.

It can attack the nerves throughout the body, producing numbness, or pain and weakness, particularly in the limbs. Indeed, this is another standard warning of Type 2 diabetes, especially numbness in the feet. If this is left to progress, the feet may deteriorate to the point that may result in the need for amputation.

It can also affect blood circulation in major and minor blood vessels, leading to an increased risk of heart failure. For the minor vessels, it can cause kidney failure and also affect the eyes. Unexplained blurred vision is yet another symptom of diabetes, and in some cases this can lead to total blindness. For the major blood vessels, it can greatly increase the risk of heart attacks and strokes.

The risk of every single one of these complications is dramatically increased by smoking.

A heightened blood sugar level, such as I had, could result in devastating complications if left untreated for years.

Diabetes trends

The International Diabetes Federation (IDF) produced a Diabetes Atlas* which quantifies the prevalence of diabetes worldwide. To outline the numbers and trends, their results for the United States and the United Kingdom are presented below. However, these trends are reflected worldwide. Even some of the countries who did not have many diabetic people in their population are beginning to show an increase, and the speed of the increase appears to be related to the incidence of fast food outlets springing up.

For the United Kingdom, the IDF reports that 6.8% of the adult population have diabetes, which includes an estimated 2.5% that are currently undiagnosed. It is estimated that another 9.8% have prediabetes.

For the United States, they report that 10.9% of the adult population have diabetes, which includes an estimated 3% that are currently undiagnosed. It is estimated that another 12.6% have prediabetes. To get an idea of the trend, the incidence of diabetes in the UK is now double what it was 20 years earlier. In the United States it is triple what it was 20 years earlier. There are predictions that both sets of numbers will continue to rise unabated.

Other countries worldwide are following a similar trend. This almost parallels the obesity trend in the previous chapter.

The statistics in these two chapters highlight an interesting point. The population of people with Type 2 diabetes who are classed as obese is more than 50%, which is a clear majority. Now, looking at the much higher percentage of the population of people classed as obese as opposed to those who are right now diagnosed with diabetes, it is clear that the population of people classed as obese who have Type 2 diabetes is a minority. There are various different ways to interpret this, and it does not negate the idea that being overweight increases the long-term risk of becoming diabetic. However, it further supports the earlier statement that the real enemy is insulin resistance, and that high insulin resistance fuels obesity at least as much as the other way round.

Either way, it is clear that the modern-day environment drives both the obesity and diabetic trends. People who become very overweight, like I was, are usually victims of this environment. It can be a great challenge to break free, and on the basis of this, a massive diet industry and culture has arisen.

But… there are choices. This book aims to provide some tools and resources for managing and even reversing Type 2 diabetes.

As a final note for this chapter, I would like to present a particularly empowering concept, and that is to outline how Type 2 diabetes can possibly be reversed.

Many people and also many doctors will tell you that once you get diabetes, you have it for life and the best you can ever do is manage and control it. This is of course true for Type 1 diabetes.

Imagine that someone who has a healthy pancreas lives the modern lifestyle and as a result their insulin resistance starts to increase. When this happens, the blood sugar level starts to increase as a direct result, and eventually rises above the thresholds in the table outlined above. If this is detected, the person is labelled as a Type 2 diabetic.

If this elevated sugar level is undetected or untreated, the pancreas could eventually wear out, and the diabetes could progress to the point where insulin is needed to maintain survival. However, if it is caught before any significant reduction in insulin production capability is made, the kind of programme in this book will help reduce insulin resistance and maintain the result. This is one reason to check out not only diabetes but also prediabetes, and nip it in the bud before it becomes established.

If on a normal day-to-day basis and living the lifestyle you have chosen for yourself results in normal blood sugar levels without the need for any medication, we could ask "Where is the diabetes?"

Thinking this way, your body was simply out of balance, and once you have restored the balance, there is no reason to regard yourself as having any kind of disease. In that sense, you have reversed the diabetes.

My blood sugar levels have been normal and stable for over ten years, and the next chapters are designed to open up new ways of thinking about the process to make it easier to achieve and maintain.

---

* International Diabetes Federation. IDF Diabetes Atlas, 5th edn. Brussels, Belgium: International Diabetes Federation, 2011

CHAPTER THREE

Mental preparations for success

Many people go on diets in order to maintain their health. Sometimes this works, but in the large majority of cases it fails. Sometimes the diet is thrown out, to be replaced by a different one. Or the dieting phase lasts only a short time. Or sometimes the weight can be shed, only to all be put back on following the brief moment of triumph. Some of you will have experienced at least one of these – I certainly did.

It would be great if there were a magic way of suddenly achieving the weight and blood sugar that you want. Unfortunately, I have not seen any evidence of this. So it is worth reflecting for a moment why so many people do not succeed.

I think it is partly because it is easy to set up short-term goals, but that does not always guarantee long-term success. In addition, the focus can be so much on the physical acts of what we eat and what exercise we do that the mental preparation for success is often overlooked.

This chapter will provide some useful ideas in this area.

My journey

I had come back from the hospital, and just wanted to get my diabetes fixed. But I had agreed with my doctor that I had three months to do some diet and exercise to reduce my blood sugar enough to start the diabetic medication he had in mind.

At this point, I did not have any mental tools in place, and did not know what to do. But I had decided to take full responsibility for managing my condition, and had to make a start somehow. Yet I was not ready to go on any kind of diet. So for the first week or two, until I had thought it out, I said to myself, "OK. I know I have been overeating. I will *continue* to overeat, but just a little less, and will start to ratchet it down as time goes on."

I also decided to join a gym as part of my agreement with the doctor to do some exercise. My son joined me for the first phase of this, and it helped me feel more supported.

But while this was all a good start, it was clearly not a strategy that would ensure any kind of long-term success.

One of the first things was to look at different diets, as that is how most people usually approach this. I was at first attracted to the idea of some diets which involved very low carbohydrate indeed, and promised reversal of diabetes. But it was controversial, and anyway that was not how I wanted to run my life. This kind of eating will be mentioned later in the book.

It was probably the visit to the hospital dietician that helped me work out how I wanted to handle this. The dietician was very pleasant. She described to me exactly what I should be eating, and what I should avoid. She clearly defined the portion sizes I should have, and of course these were frighteningly smaller than what I usually ate. It was all good solid advice, and technically there was absolutely nothing wrong with it. In spite of that, as I left her office, I knew that I was not going to follow the guidelines she had suggested. To me, it was like facing a prison sentence, and I wanted – no, I *demanded* – the freedom to eat what I wanted. It was very clear what I didn't want, and yet something had to change. So now it was time to think as creatively as I could what I *did* want, and find a way to succeed.

One place to start was to ask what the reasons behind my past failures were. One common theme was that every action had been short-term, with absolutely no maintenance strategy in place. I had just jumped into a diet to lose weight, with little thought of how what I was doing fitted into my life, or how I could possibly maintain it once I had succeeded.

With this in mind, I built in a long-term maintenance part to describe what I wanted. For me, the decision to define success by weight and blood sugar felt right. So I came up with the mission statement below:

> 66 *I will attain a weight of 85 kilograms and a normal fasting blood sugar level, and maintain it easily, healthily and naturally for the rest of my life.* 99

Note this is not a goal in the usual sense of the word, and it will be discussed further later in this chapter. It immediately set up a long-term perspective. At that point, I realised with a shock that I had absolutely no long-term plan in life at all, and perhaps at some unconscious level I knew the danger I was in.

Actually, I wanted even more than this. I wished I could eat what I wanted with very little need for discipline, control or restriction. At first, this simply seemed like a fantasy, an impossible dream. The food I liked and the quantities I was eating, and also my sedentary exercise-avoiding lifestyle, were responsible for my current situation. How would it be if I simply learned to like different foods, enjoyed activity more, and became totally satisfied after eating a more appropriate quantity of food?

So, with these outcomes in mind, I asked "What has to be true for this to succeed?"

Firstly, I wanted to change the way I thought about hunger. It currently consisted of two states: 'being full up' or 'being hungry', and this was driving some very poor eating decisions. My strategy here was to create some very useful distinctions, and this is described in detail in the next chapter. I also decided that if I chose to allow myself to reach the point of feeling slightly hungry, it was not about being on a diet. It would be more about preparing my mind and body so that I could operate more easily and naturally in the future.

Secondly, it was important to be able to have unhealthy foods such as cake and chocolate in my house and be able to live comfortably with this. I also wanted to be able to go to social occasions, parties and buffets, and still maintain my outcome without feeling restricted. The only way to achieve this was to change how I thought about the kind of food that used to tempt me to overeat in the past. I spent some time imagining what it might be like to be able to have them there and simply feel neutral about them, and not having to resist them at all. Or taking a small amount if I fancied and being able to stop after that.

Thirdly, even at this point it was clear that there is a fundamental change of thinking when the initial target is achieved. Before reaching the target, success can be thought of as making a noticeable or measurable difference. With the passage of time, there is maybe a smaller clothes size, a lower weight, a lower blood sugar reading.

However, after reaching the target, success is defined as staying the same. As a result, the motivation for continuing the success phase is somewhat different from that of the maintenance phase. There are many people who go on a diet, and achieve their goal, only to go back to their original weight or even higher.

The desired outcome was to maintain the success easily and naturally. Habits are a force to maintain sameness, and of course habits can be friends or foes. Sometimes habits just seem to happen for no reason of their own. I decided to make sure the right habits were built in as a continuing process. So I asked "What habits do I *want* to have in place to support me once I achieve the desired result?"

As one example, it was a habit to buy a large bar of chocolate from the machine almost every day when working at the office. If I had broken it just by abstaining, I would have been fighting myself and feeling deprived. Indeed, I would have spent so much time thinking about *not* eating chocolate that it would have interfered with everything else, and spending time thinking about *not* doing something often has the opposite effect than is intended. So I decided to see if I could develop a new habit, and that was to always have available the kind of food I could eat in almost unlimited quantity, and learn to eat that in preference. This would be food that was savoury as opposed to being sweet, as that was another habit I decided I wanted to change. So I kept large quantities of food such as celery, tomatoes, mushrooms, or vegetable juice right by my side, and always available. When I felt the urge to eat, I started on what I had, and continued until my jaws got tired, or until the desire went away. If necessary, this could happen many times a day. Eventually it was no longer a habit to eat the chocolate. Interestingly, that new habit lasted for about a year, and it gradually ended up just being a small snack every now and then. I chose to let it change as it had permanently served its original purpose. That new habit *is* a good long-term prospect to help ensure a natural and voluntary adherence to maintaining the result when the time came.

I then took it a little further. I liked certain foods, and was at best neutral to some better eating choices. So I dared to ask the question "What food do I *want* to like?" Broccoli was a case in point, and I had never been attracted to it in the past. What could I creatively find about broccoli to like? I was aware that I had been thinking 'Mmmm, I love the warm moist taste of fried chicken'; and when I tried broccoli, thought to myself in exactly the same tone 'Mmmm, I love the cool crisp crunch of broccoli.' I also got to appreciate the dark green colour, the interesting texture and even the smell. After about a month I got to actually like both raw and lightly cooked broccoli, and also other foods I chose to start to like. As a result, my choices were increasing as I got to like an increasing variety of healthy foods.

Fourthly, I refused to use the word 'diet' at any point along the way. A diet is something you go on, and come off. I didn't want anything to get in the way of the decision for this to be a permanent change. When people asked me "How are you doing with your diet?" I didn't say or even *think* "I am not on a diet" but instead let the word go past and simply smiled and said "My lifestyle change is going well."

At the same time, I started to think about doing a similar thing with exercise. My personal decision was for about half the weight loss to come from how I ate, and half from exercise. I then made a distinction between the kind of activity that naturally fits in with daily life, and the activity that needs time set aside to do. For daily life, I built in new habits. Whenever I saw stairs and an escalator next to each other, I took the stairs. Indeed, I now feel compelled to do it, and my habit of running up the stairs even when I am with other people can be quite annoying for them. But this habit did not happen by chance, and I intentionally chose it. As habits I chose, almost without thinking, I take stairs instead of the lift, run up escalators instead of standing still, walk briskly instead of my previous dawdle, and a host of others.

In addition to that, I made time to do exercise, usually but not necessarily at the gym. As someone who was very unfit, I thought that all I wanted was to increase my level of fitness to enable me to exert an extra few hundred calories per day, and also to burn up the excess sugar in my blood. At that point, I hadn't fully understood about insulin resistance, and how important exercise is in reducing this resistance. But it didn't matter, as it was the right decision anyway. Eventually something very positive happened that I didn't expect, which will be described in the final chapter.

Next, it was time to think ahead and do a little mental exercise, imagining the future in lots of different ways. How will my lifestyle change fit in with my family, or people I spend time with? How will I handle a lapse, such as an eating binge or an increase in weight? Will I like the person I will become? Is there anything I would not like about the change and what could I put in place to handle it? How do I want to behave at a buffet?

All of these are important questions. For each, I imagined what it would be like, what I actually wanted, and changed what it would be like until I was happy with it. One example was that I used to hate buying clothes. I remember often going to a suit shop and only having three drab suits of my size to choose from, and finding it a depressing experience. More often than not, I walked out without buying anything. A significant weight loss would not only cost money, but make me have to go out and buy clothes all over again.

The perspective I chose to adopt was that firstly buying new clothes was a sign of success, secondly I had an increasing level of choice, thirdly the clothes would be less expensive, and finally I would look better. When it was time to change almost every item of clothing as a result of my decreasing size, I was ready to embrace and enjoy the experience. Both times.

A very important part of the process, especially at the beginning, was that if I wanted to make a change, I would imagine doing it not only immediately, but also well into the future. If I did not feel good about doing it in the long term, it was time to try to understand what was causing that and think through how to change it so that it did feel good. The act of imagining doing it in the long term helped prepare my brain to adopt and continue it, and as a result already increased my chance of success. Also any editing process helped ensure that I had made the best possible and most long-lasting decision.

It would be nice to be able to say that I had all of this worked out from the very beginning. However, this wouldn't be true. I started with no idea of how to succeed, except that this time I would set it up to succeed in the long term. The process of setting this up took months, and continued to evolve as I encountered new challenges and experiences. If I was ever going to succeed, this was my best chance, as I had put a lot of powerful mental tools in place as a solid foundation for dealing with the Type 2 diabetes diagnosis.

I was now ready to see how closely I could get to my target weight and blood sugar.

Setting up for long-term success

One thing is certain: if you are facing any risk of becoming diabetic, or have already passed that point, something has to change in your life. That is likely to mean a change in how you eat, and what level of activity you have.

The first thought is often to go on a diet. The word 'diet' is commonly associated with things like self-starvation, discipline, deprivation and restriction of choice. In some ways, that can be like paddling upstream. With strength and determination, it can be done and there are people who indeed do this. One reason some people don't succeed is when for any reason you stop paddling at any point along the way, you are automatically pulled back by the current towards where you started.

So the philosophy of this chapter is to help build mental resources, which effectively help to reduce or even reverse the direction of the stream, so that it becomes less effort to achieve in the first place, and maintain in the long run. This actually provides you in the end with more choices rather than fewer. So, this will be presented in a way that aligns with the way the brain works, and the more we do that, the more downstream the journey will become.

One thing that is important to understand in advance is that, at an unconscious level, the brain does not understand the word 'no', or other negations such as *not, don't* or *won't*. A good example of this at work is if an anxious adult sees a child walking on top of a wall. The immediate impulse is to say something like "Don't fall!" At this point, the child had not even thought about falling. The only way the brain can process this is to imagine falling, and then negate – by which time it is probably too late. A more brain-friendly way to do this is to say something like "Be sure to keep your balance," but we don't usually do this.

Why is this important? If you decide that you *don't* want to be your current weight, or you *won't* eat that piece of cake, or *not* watch television every night, a part of your brain gets the exact opposite message. Just like the child walking on the wall. So it is important to decide what you actually *do* want, and express it in a positive way that will help you to achieve it. Let us work through a couple of examples.

"I want to lose weight and reduce my blood sugar" is surely a common desire. Sometimes, when driving near a roundabout, there are road signs that instruct 'Reduce speed now' which is really quite inappropriate when the traffic is slow and the car is actually stationary. It doesn't really have any end or criteria for success, and is not likely to be the best way to start. There are more effective ways to describe what you want than to simply use words like lose and reduce.

Many people like to make goals to aim at, which are usually targets that can be measured and achieved, with a definite end-point and usually a fixed timescale. Goals certainly can make it easy to focus on what one is trying to achieve. So the next example is "I want to be 80 kilograms by July 15th so that I look good on the beach." Imagine it is actually achievable, and within the person's ability to do so, and also that it is ecological in that it is in that person's health interest to become that weight. This is a great goal, and could easily help this person have a very enjoyable holiday. However, it has an end, and you might wonder what would motivate that person to continue any programme once the holiday was over. Some people go through this kind of cycle every year. So, although this is better than the example in the paragraph above, it is not necessarily the kind of wish that will lead to long-term success.

Indeed, what I suggest is strictly speaking not a goal, but more of a direction. A goal has a well-defined end-point and a timescale, and a direction is open-ended and sets a path forward, possibly for a lifetime – a little like gravity, always acting on you no matter where in the process you are.

The first thing is to be clear what your criteria are. For me it was weight and blood sugar. If a lower weight is a part of what you want to achieve, it is important to aim initially for a weight that is both healthy and achievable, and some ideas on this will be described later. For others it may be clothes size, fitness level, or even other things.

The kind of wish I would suggest is something like "I want to be <whatever criteria you wish>, and maintain it easily and naturally for the rest of my life."

Setting it up so that this is for the rest of your life certainly puts a different perspective on the kind of decisions you take, and also on handling little lapses and glitches that are bound to happen along the way.

What do you want?

It is useful to clarify some things in advance, in order to help you make the best choices, and also that you deal with any internal and external potential saboteurs. So it is worth spending some time thinking through the questions below, as a guide.

There will be many places in this book where it is suggested that you imagine how life would be for you under a different set of circumstances. For each of these, you will get the most benefit by entering a nice relaxed, open state of body and mind. As this is an important part of setting up your future success, it is worth spending just a few minutes to prepare for this, to provide the very best chance of working towards your success. The best time to do this is when you know you will not be disturbed by any external event, and when there is no time pressure on you. Find a quiet place where you can sit, lie, or put yourself in a very comfortable position. If you want music in the background, a good choice might be slow relaxing music which is purely instrumental, so there are no external words to distract your thinking. For some people, slow Baroque music from Accelerated Learning music collections can provide a useful background. Once you are comfortable and are breathing slowly and deeply, it is good to remember a quiet and pleasant experience. Were you in a beautiful environment? What pleasant sounds and smells can you remember? How did it feel? Spend a short while there, and then bring your mind back to the present, ready to imagine how the future can be for you.

Once you are in this relaxed state, imagine what it would be like some time after you have reached the target, and been maintaining it almost without effort for a period of time. How would you feel about yourself? From that perspective, and enjoying looking back over the path you took to succeed, consider to what extent all the time and effort you put in would have been worth it. Would you like the kind of person you would become if you achieved all this? What specifically would you like about it?

Are there any parts of it you would dislike, or have doubts about?

There was a programme on television featuring someone who had lost an incredible amount of weight, and even became a fitness guru. He admitted that he became arrogant, promiscuous and selfish, and did not like the kind of person he had become. His wife echoed the sentiment. After a while, he put all the weight back on again. In a follow-up interview, he said that he loved his food too much, and he wasn't yet ready to slim down again. It is possible, and his stated view, that this was due to his love of food. However, I suspect strongly that the fact he did not like the person he had become could have played a major role in totally sabotaging his success. He would probably retain all his weight until he could create an image of someone he would like and respect if he were ever to do it again.

So, as you imagine the new and successful you, is there anything you would change about that person? How would you want that person to behave, and how would it feel from the inside to behave in that way?

A slightly different question is what costs, or losses, would there be in succeeding? Are there any hidden benefits or pay-offs in not changing? I used to have an identity as a large person, often enjoying making jokes about my size. That would be gone forever. I now have a new identity as someone who has transformed from being large to being slim, and I like that a lot more. Similarly, there may be the prospect of facing the expense of buying new clothes. Or perhaps as a parent being called up to participate at a school sports day, or generate expectations from others that you can currently hide from. If issues such as these are anticipated and acknowledged, and thought through in advance how to best deal with them, they are less likely to get in the way of your success.

There will be a lot of people who will be very supportive. There may also be a few who are not, and this is worth preparing for as it could be a shock if and when it happens. Becoming slimmer and fitter could affect the balance and dynamics of a relationship, or there may be friends or work colleagues who suddenly feel threatened. Maybe a work colleague has until now enjoyed cheap taunts at your expense, and as you progress the balance changes and can even reverse. So be ready, maybe even pre-rehearse, taking it in your stride if there are any less than kind or helpful comments as you are trying to achieve your goals. If this should happen, maybe you can even smile to yourself as it is a sign of how much you have changed.

Finally, as part of clarifying what you want, it is also worth making a strong representation of *why* you want it. If there was a trigger, a threshold you passed, that propelled you to action, take the time to reflect on it. For some, it is the onset of a health shock, such as a heart attack or diagnosis or warning of diabetes. For others it may be a desire to see children or grandchildren grow up, or to be a better example to the family. For others still, it may be a threshold experience of a taunt or insult too far, or a resounding "No!" when looking in the mirror or stepping on the scales. Or simply a desire to be healthy, and a wish to avoid disease.

Whatever the reasons, it is a lifetime journey you are embarking on now, and these are useful resources to always have with you, as a reminder of why you started doing this when you need that little bit of extra motivation to keep going.

It has been said that one can endure any 'what' if there is a good enough 'why'. So it is worth the effort to build and maintain for yourself a truly compelling 'why'.

When you have done this, and clarified what you really want and why you want it, you have already started to set yourself up to succeed. The next chapter presents a collection of mental resources, organised into ten strategies, to help you succeed even further.

CHAPTER FOUR

Ten mental strategies for long-term success

At this point, let's remind ourselves of the desired outcome, which is to make whatever change you have decided is appropriate, and to maintain it easily and naturally for the rest of your life.

This can initially appear to be a very challenging task, as it probably takes you to a different set of behaviours, beliefs and values than you had before. It certainly did for me.

The aim of this chapter is to help build up your resources to make it easier to achieve and maintain your success. As there are a lot of different resources and tools, I have organised them into ten different strategies to help you succeed, once you have fully clarified what you want as described in the previous chapter.

Some of these ideas may appeal to you more than others at first, and I would recommend that this chapter be re-read and reviewed as you progress through your programme.

Here are the ten principles, followed by an explanation of each in greater detail:

1 *Maintain a long-tem perspective*
Never impose anything on yourself that you cannot maintain in the long term

2 *Choose and adopt habits to support your goals*
Decide what habits you want to adopt to help support your success

3 *Build in distinctions to help expand your choices*
Get to recognise different kinds of hunger

4 *Don't stop – swap!*
Rather than deprive yourself, choose wisely when to do something else

5 *Ratchet your way to success*
Expand your comfort zone by going very slightly outside of it

6 *Nothing is forbidden*
Set yourself up to make wise choices, rather than "I can't have this!"

7 *Take it slowly and steadily*
Don't skip meals or starve

8 *Be gentle with yourself, giving rewards often*
Give yourself the support and kind words that a close friend would give you

9 *Make sure the new you is someone you like and respect*
Treat yourself and others with respect, and choose your labels carefully

10 *Embrace all experiences to build your resources*
Even bad experiences and failures can give you more strength to succeed

1   Maintain a long-term perspective

The first and probably most important step has already been taken if your statement contains the wording relating to the rest of your life. Taking such a perspective opens up some interesting and powerful possibilities.

The first is that unless your health is currently at dire and immediate risk due to weight or high sugar levels, it does not matter in the long term how fast or how slowly you progress, as long as you do progress. In fact, your body will make a lot of complex adjustments throughout the whole achievement phase, and in spite of some of the heroics we see with weight-losing races on the television, there is a benefit in approaching this slowly and steadily. One reason is that what you want to lose is fat, and not muscle or water. Many fad diets that claim to take weight off fast may actually reduce water and muscle as well, and prime the body to store fat more effectively.

This is where a long-term perspective helps. For someone who is 80 pounds overweight, it can take well over a year to achieve the target. In my case, I started at just over 1.5 pounds a week and this slowed down the closer I got to the target. So it took me well over a year. I am really not a very patient person, and of course would have liked to do it much more quickly, but it was a healthier way to do it and set up a lifestyle I could maintain relatively easily. It was only through having a long-term perspective that helped me plan and achieve it. Interestingly, looking back from a distance, it now feels like it happened quite quickly. There are many diet books that promise you faster results, but they might not help you maintain it for ever.

Having said this, there is nothing wrong with having timescaled goals. Indeed, some goal-orientation can be very motivating, and help keep the programme on track. If you are aiming to reduce by an average of say a pound a week, then maybe an appropriate mini-goal would be at the end of every month, or maybe after ten weeks. You can of course celebrate when you achieve each of them.

Another useful way to benefit from a long-term perspective is to think what you are prepared to do in order to achieve and maintain the result. For example, the cultivation of a new and useful habit, such as choosing to walk up stairs whenever there is a choice, or the swapping out of one kind of eating to a different one. Whatever the intended new habit is, it is beneficial to imagine doing it for a month, for a year, and also in the long term. If this feels comfortable and you are prepared to do it, then that is a good time to take the step. If there is something that feels wrong, or you express any doubts, or just can't see yourself maintaining it, this is a time to adjust it in whatever way works for you, so that it fits into your life. There are lots of creative ways to do that, ranging from ramping it up more slowly, or doing it only in certain contexts, or making some specific exceptions you are happy with. For example, you might choose to drink sparkling water instead of wine, but not when you are at weddings and parties, or only on Mondays and Wednesdays. Then, when you are totally at ease with the idea, start actually doing it.

This has two advantages. Firstly, simply imagining it in the long term sets a direction for the brain. This can help you adopt the change more automatically. Secondly, you never impose something that does not fit into your life and that you cannot or do not wish to maintain.

Yet another reason a long-term perspective is helpful is to help handle lapses in a resilient way. I have known of smokers who have given up for six months, had one cigarette, and then decided they were failures because they had a lapse, and started smoking again. Somehow, that one cigarette was more important and significant to them than the fact that they had been successful in stopping for six months. They let a lapse become a relapse, and lead to a total collapse.

It is common, indeed expected, to have lapses. I certainly did, and there are many times when having set a direction, something exceptional happened and I ate far more than I wanted, or skipped a planned exercise session. Like the smoker, one could say "Oh no! I have totally failed. I give up." On the other hand, let us suppose that one day for whatever reason you ate an extra 3,000 calories, which is the equivalent of six 100g bars of chocolate, or a really huge Indian or Chinese meal. How can one think about that positively? The way I did it was to tell myself something like "This is less than one pound, and at worst will only put the programme back a few days or maybe a week. On the scale of things, this is just a blip." No failure – and certainly no collapse.

Finally, to maintain the long-term perspective, it is useful to always have in mind the trigger that spurred you to action, and the reasons why you are doing this. Being able to recall it at any time, especially when things start to feel a little uphill or difficult, can be a resource to keep you going. It might help to make a mental symbol you can bring up to remind you, or a sound or special word, or even a feeling or a movement you don't usually make, such as touching two fingers together in a way you don't usually do. Or even better, any combination of these. The ability to quickly and frequently bring to mind what actually triggered you to action, and the reasons why you started the journey, is a useful asset to help you all the way along the journey.

2   Choose and adopt habits to support your goals

There are two very different phases of the journey.

The first is the Achievement phase, which is usually the phase that dieters focus on. There is something special about making visible progress every week or maybe every month. Another few pounds less, or maybe a clothes size smaller. Or lower blood sugar. Or perhaps people will comment on how much better you are looking. Each step along the way can be something to celebrate, to feel proud of, perhaps to tick off another goal. For many people, this kind of success is highly motivating. The desire for this success can keep people on track.

Once the target is close to being achieved, there is nothing wrong with reviewing it and checking whether you are happy with it. The achievement stage can pick up again if you decide it is in your health interests to go that little bit further. Throughout this phase, success is defined as having progressed in some way to your final desired state.

Once the final target is achieved, then you are in the Maintenance phase. The thinking here is quite different, and so is the source of motivation. Success is now defined as being the same this month as you were last month. Some people are much happier in the first phase, and others are happier in the second phase. It is less common to find people equally happy and motivated in both. The net result is that there is a danger of a change of motivation, and this can be where some people fail. The very success of reaching the target can in fact be the start of the cessation of the whole programme.

If we think ahead and know in advance that sooner or later we will be facing this, we can do something about it from the beginning. One important decision is to make sure we cultivate habits that will keep us going right into and through the maintenance phase. If those new habits support a lifestyle that maintains the target, then this is like paddling downstream. It takes less effort, you don't have to be paddling all the time, and the maintenance phase becomes a lot easier. We still always need to be checking where the currents are taking us, and make appropriate corrections to make sure we are always heading in the right direction, but this is much easier than continuing to paddle upstream.

The time to put those habits in place is not when the maintenance phase starts. It is best if the habits are already developed by then. The diagram illustrates the general idea.

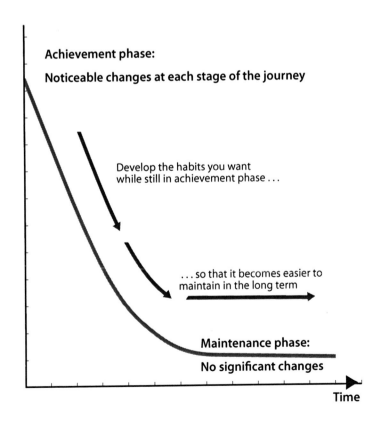

Achievement phase:
Noticeable changes at each stage of the journey

Develop the habits you want
while still in achievement phase . . .

. . . so that it becomes easier to
maintain in the long term

Maintenance phase:
No significant changes

Time

In everyday life, it is easy to develop habits at random. It has been said "The chains of habit are too weak to be felt until they are too strong to be broken." What I am going to suggest is to find a quiet time, maybe as outlined in the previous chapter, and simply ask yourself "What habits would I *like* to have in order to support what I want to achieve?" It is a good idea initially to put aside whether those habits seem possible or not and simply think through what would have to be different for you to live from day to day, easily and naturally, maintaining your success. What foods would you like to like, even if you don't yet enjoy them right now? What activities would you like to be doing to make sure that insulin resistance is a thing of the past?

I also suggest doing this with the thought that once new habits are adopted, it may then be easier to consider replacing old habits. It may even happen spontaneously. As the saying goes, the chains of habit are hard to break, and trying to confront every one of them and simply breaking them by force or discipline is not easy for many people. Instead, build the habits you want, and it will be easier to exchange the old habits for the new ones.

It has been said that it takes 21 days to create a new habit by doing it daily, once the action is actually started. Some habits can take anything from a week to months to become established. Here are just a few ideas to help build your own new habits.

Old habit	New habit
Eat three meals a day, taking large portions just in case you get hungry later	Eat more times a day, and be confident about having smaller portions
Hungry? Get one or two bars of chocolate from the machine, or a large cheeseburger and chips. Still hungry – eat more! And straight away	Hungry? Eat the celery, tomatoes, banana, fish, chicken breast or whatever you have brought with you. Still hungry – eat more! Or wait 20 minutes to see if body signals satisfaction
Hungry, but want to drink? Get a chocolate drink from the machine, or a sugared fizzy drink, perhaps two or three times a day	Hungry, but want to drink? Chilled water can be very refreshing and often satisfying. Or have some vegetable juice, or unsugared coffee or tea
Tired? Slump down and watch television, or sprawl on the settee and play a game on your computer	Tired? It takes a bit of effort at first, but get out of the house. Dance, walk, afterwards go to the gym, or play a sport, or just do work on the house or garden
At hotel, work or department store, take the lift to the floor you wish to go to	Find the steps and take them. If you need to get to the tenth floor, just climb as many flights as you think appropriate, and take the lift the rest of the way
I love the soft moist taste of pizza/fried chicken/cake	I love the cool crisp crunch of celery/cucumber, or the refreshing taste of fruit/vegetable juice
Go to coffee bar with friends every day. Have a large latte	Go to coffee bar with friends every day. Have a large black unsugared coffee

51

Only you know what habits will work best for you, and in what contexts. So feel free to make a totally different list.

How do you build in new habits? New tastes? And new ways of thinking? This will be different for different people. I would like to offer a powerful way of thinking even before we look at some of the more subtle ways of adopting new habits, and one that does not necessarily need the belief or confidence that it is easy or possible to achieve. Taking the example of the swap from latte to black unsugared coffee, it might be easy to feel this is a step that cannot be taken, or that you haven't yet got the confidence that such a step will be successful. So what would happen if you decided to behave and think **as if** you already liked black coffee and had already adopted it as a habit? Perhaps ordering it without any hesitation, **as if** this is what you really wanted. Perhaps greeting the new sensation of the slightly more bitter taste of the coffee **as if** you already really liked it, and smiling at your friends as you drink it. Of course, it does not have to be coffee and it could apply to any habit you would like to adopt. For some people, acting **as if** any barrier you see in front of you is already overcome might be an interesting way to initiate a new habit that you choose to help underpin your long-term success.

The next few sections may provide a range of ideas to help create a good foundation for you to build up for yourself an arsenal of ideas and tools to help you achieve this.

3   Build in distinctions to help expand your choices

One way to approach building in new habits, and indeed expanding your freedom to make choices, is to enrich the distinctions you are able to make, and increase your range of awareness.

Let us take an example. Imagine that the only words you had for relationships were 'friend' and 'enemy'. On that basis, people are either with you or against you, and you would end up with a poor selection of relationships. Indeed, this would drive your behaviour, tolerance of other people and your whole attitude to social interaction. Of course, we also have words like acquaintance and many others. It is interesting how wisdom and maturity can emerge from continuing to enrich the distinctions.

Some Inuit languages have a single word meaning 'I like you very much, but I would not go seal-hunting with you'. Consider the effect of having such a word in your vocabulary, or at least having such a concept that is easily brought to mind; or even better if you had an even wider range of words or concepts with that level of richness. This would certainly increase your flexibility and ability to make and maintain a far richer set of relationships in a way that maintains acceptance and respect for a wider variety of people.

Now imagine that the only eating concepts you had were 'being full up' or 'being hungry'. On that basis, you are either totally stuffed, or want to eat. This can end up with a very poor selection of habits and decisions. Indeed, this would – and did – drive my eating behaviour, my compulsion to eat, and my whole attitude to food.

So, in a similar way to the Inuit seal-hunting concept, it might be interesting to build a palette of different kinds of hunger. With a little practice and experience, you may become able to identify each one of them quickly when they occur.

I would like to present a few examples, just to help get the process started. It doesn't matter whether any of them apply to you. What is important is that your list contains real distinctions that fit with your experience. I would recommend starting with at least five different ones, and preferably more. Indeed, the more the better.

Which of these can you relate to, and also what other ones can you come up with?

- I have eaten enough that I will be satisfied in 20 minutes from now
- This is the kind of hunger I get when I am actually thirsty for water
- This is the kind of hunger I get when I am bored
- I have just seen it/smelt it
- If I don't eat this, I fear I will miss out
- This is genuine hunger, signalling that I need to eat right now
- I want food for comfort, and I want it now
- I really want a taste of this, and would be happy with just a little of it

Note that one could simply ask "Why do I want to eat this right now?" Some people advocate this kind of analysis, introspection and even self-therapy. However, the 'why' question often results in searching for justification or plausible excuses, and that is not always helpful. The nice thing about simply identifying the kind of hunger is that once it is acknowledged, you can set it up so that you still have a choice and are totally free to take it.

Once you have this kind of list, and can relate at least one real experience to each item on the list, you are ready. If you want to set up a habit, then at least for the first few weeks, every time you want to eat something, simply pause and ask yourself "What kind of hunger is this?" and let the answer come to you. Then simply ask "What choice do I want to make right now?"

Suppose you were walking past a cake shop, and you saw an item you know you liked. In the past, you may have simply gone in and bought it. Now, you can ask yourself these questions. The answer might be "I want this anyway today." Or maybe "I want it today, and will be happy to walk past next time." The difference is that you are now interrupting the automatic 'see it – want it' reaction, and creating a little space to start making a conscious and mindful choice. It doesn't always have to be a good choice, but it is now *your* choice.

Note that the first two items on the list have some real biological basis. Earlier, during the brief description of the anatomy of a meal, it was mentioned that it typically takes 20 minutes for the satisfaction signal to be fully established. With that knowledge, one can finish a meal with what feels like a small amount of appetite still remaining, and yet still feel satisfied after 20 minutes – especially if the meal is one that does not trigger a surge of insulin, which is a topic that will be described in the next chapter.

Some people advocate drinking water in order to trick your body into thinking it has eaten well. While the tactic may be useful, I certainly would not recommend adopting this underlying philosophy. It is far better to treat the mind and body as a fully co-operating unit, and not play any kind of trickery. The way I consider this is that sometimes when the body needs water it sends a signal that can be mistaken for hunger. If that is the case, it is worth trying out drinking some water to see whether this is where the hunger feelings come from. If you are right, this has helped you progress. If you are wrong, then you will still feel the hunger say 20 minutes later, and can revisit the process. Either way you will have learned something, and increased the effectiveness of this resource.

After a while, this whole process becomes more automatic, and kicks in even without you having to try. This is independent of what choices you actually made, as it is the awareness that you have been working on. Hopefully, some of your choices will have aligned with what you want to achieve, and this is a very good first step towards setting up not only to achieve your target, but also to maintain it more effortlessly in the future.

There are plenty of creative ways to enhance this, and I would like to outline two more below.

Imagine that for something like a cake you have identified the kind of hunger, and decided you would like to eat it anyway, even though you know it might not be an optimum decision. Then it is worth asking "How will I feel in one to two hours from now if I go ahead?" You will know from past experience how you will feel. It might be guilty, or bloated, or totally satisfied. It is also really worth becoming aware of energy crashes that may have happened one to two hours following a high-sugar snack, and being able to relate the two. Remember, this is not just a question. It is best done as an explicit memory of how it actually felt when this happened in the past, and if possible also what you were saying to yourself at the time.

If you think you will feel satisfied and happy that you ate it, go ahead and enjoy it. My experience is that this whole process did not restrict me from doing anything I wanted, but it did help me make choices which were mindful rather than just reacting, and helped me progress.

Note that a similar process could also be applied to inactivity. Have you ever had a time where you were just sitting doing nothing, or maybe just watching television to see whatever was on? And then somehow overcame it, and once you were 'up and running' felt a lot better for it. But the transition needed to overcome some inertia. Yet there are times when it is totally appropriate to do no activity. So, based on this process, if inactivity is something you also want to address, enriching the answers to "What kind of inactivity is this?" in a parallel way could be very worthwhile.

Another issue some people may have that can affect their success is stress. A good first step is to simply recognise it, especially if it is contributing to a desire to eat something that in the long term you don't want to be eating, or is affecting a decision to do some exercise. Some stresses appear to be due to external pressures, such as any activity which you are told has to be completed by a certain date. Some stresses appear to be due to expectations from others to conform or behave in some way, or to do something to a high standard. And some will be from judgments made by yourself on what you should or should not do. If this is an important issue for you, then it is worth taking time to make five or even ten distinctions, including as many as you can that are generated from inside yourself. Then when periods of stress do occur, it would be useful to assign it to one of your categories in order to increase your awareness of which kind of stress you might be experiencing.

There may be many other areas of your life where you could apply this kind of process.

One more food-oriented distinction I would like to offer is based on something I noticed I was doing often, especially with drinks but also with food. Before I started to enjoy drinking water, I used to drink a lot of fizzy drinks, or orange juice, or milk. The first taste would of course let me know what I was drinking, and then I gulped the rest down and never really noticed the taste any more. Did this also apply to food? Early in my programme, when eating something I enjoyed, I checked out whether the tenth mouthful was as satisfying as the first, from a taste point of view. In general, it wasn't. To be fair, there have been a very few exceptions, especially when eating very slowly. If one of the things you want to do is to change the amount that you are eating, especially when it is on the plate in front of you, this might also be a useful distinction.

There is another step to enhance this process even further, or which can also serve as a good alternative, and which will be covered next.

4   Don't stop – swap!

As mentioned earlier, at an unconscious level the brain does not understand the word 'no'. The harder you try not to think about something, the less likely you are to succeed. How do you know right now that you are not thinking about a purple sprout of broccoli? And if you are, how are you going to stop?

That is one of the challenges we face when we are trying to stop doing something. Back to the child walking on the wall, the thought 'I must be careful not to fall' is far more likely to have an unfortunate result than 'I need to keep my balance and walk to the other end'.

How does this work with chocolate cake, fried chicken, or whatever it is that you would like to move away from? The thought 'I can't have this chocolate cake' or 'I won't eat this chocolate cake' is not as helpful as you might like it to be. So one way that can work well is to divert the thought, perhaps with a decision statement such as "I would rather..." or with a question like "What would I like to do instead?" Note the 'do' as opposed to the 'eat'. If the desire to eat is out of boredom or not feeling good, diverting to an interesting or absorbing activity may be the most useful choice, and the most appropriate habitual response to aim to build in.

Remembering the strategy in the previous section about making the distinction "What kind of hunger is this?" the question "What do I want to do instead?" might be an appropriate follow-up question to add when you know the kind of hunger is from boredom or for comfort. Or it could be an alternative strategy.

Suppose you really fancied a large chocolate bar, or a double cheeseburger. Each of these works out at a little over 500 kcal. Calories will be described in a little more detail in the next chapter. However, in addition to the amount of calories, neither of these is in line with achieving the target, and in addition is likely to produce an insulin surge and you might end up not feeling any better two hours later.

You can try to fight it – and many people succeed, at least at first. However, if you prefer to set up something that will make things easier in the future, you could imagine what you might prefer to be eating instead, even if it is initially a slight pull to divert the desire from the original food.

As an illustration, you could have two medium eggs, half a medium avocado, a small banana, four strawberries and 100 grams of cherries if you really wanted them all, and still be eating no more calories than the chocolate. However, in terms of providing healthy nutrients to the body and lower blood sugar peaks, this would be a far better choice. Here is how it looks:

Now suppose that you are looking to reduce your calorie intake a little, and that you were in the habit of eating a 100g chocolate bar every day. There were some days I used to do far worse than this. Even if you wanted a slightly sweeter choice than the example above, for example a banana, an apple and eight strawberries, you are actually eating 250 kcal less than if you had had the chocolate or cheeseburger. Here is how it looks:

Let us summarise what we have explored so far, and apply it to the chocolate bar. Once it becomes a habit to think like this, there are of course a range of choices. So if you have the chocolate every day, swap it out a few times a week as a good start. Or choose to have only a small piece of it. Or swap it for something else as in the above examples. Or decide that this is the kind of hunger that has arisen from boredom or comfort and choose to do something else instead. All of these are choices that take you in the right direction towards succeeding in your goals.

5   Ratchet your way to success

The body is a complex mechanism, and is designed to respond very protectively to sudden changes. It is also very adaptable, and changes progressively in the face of new challenges it is presented with, especially with respect to physical activity. All good exercise programmes are based on this.

In addition, it adapts to any new set of demands that are placed on it, but slowly. If it suddenly senses that there is not enough food for it to survive, it tries to protect you by conserving fat more efficiently from any food it gets. Perhaps even worse, instead of the body using up the fat when it wants energy, it starts to consume the muscle instead. This is the very opposite of what a person aiming at becoming both slimmer and more healthy wants to achieve!

Once you have firmly made the decision to become fitter and healthier, it is totally understandable that you may want results quickly. However, your body will not thank you for fast heroic-style weight loss, and it is quite respectable to reduce your weight by one to two pounds a week.

Remember, above two pounds a week and your body really starts to fight back. This book is about achieving success without suffering and at the same time increasing your health. So, introduce changes slowly, and increase them slowly too. Then just continue the process of increasing the changes. I call this the 'ratchet principle.'

The ratchet principle is a way of working that builds on success, and does not make you start on inappropriate or even unsafe levels of exercise or following restrictive diet sheets. It is very simple: start by making a small change and once it is made, keep it. A little later, make another small change, and keep doing this. For a lifestyle change, this goes on forever.

There is another reason why thinking in terms of ratcheting is important. For people who choose to lose a lot of weight, their calorie requirement is much higher at the beginning than towards the end.

If you succeed in reducing your calorie balance by say 500 kcal/day, you will almost certainly start to lose a pound a week. However, for every ten pounds you lose, you require 100 kcal a day fewer. This suggests that when you have lost 50 pounds, you will not lose any more weight unless something else changes. So if you are aiming to be more than 50 pounds lighter, something else *must* change for you to be successful. This may be offset to some extent by factors that work in your favour – if you have more muscle, and are eating more healthily, your metabolic rate will have increased somewhat, and a 50-pound reduction might mean less than a 500 kcal/day lowering of requirement. If you are more active, you will also burn more, and it is possible that your appetite will have decreased.

What this means is that a choice to adopt a particular but constant eating and exercise balance from the outset usually involves immediately imposing a level of reduction and change that is appropriate for the end stages, but restrictive and punishing at the beginning. Suddenly reducing by say 2,000 kcal a day can be too much suffering to endure willingly. In contrast, the ratchet principle is to make a small but definite change to start with, slowly increasing it as both you and your body get used to it, changing on the way down to acknowledge and deal with the diminishing requirements of the body as it slims down.

I think that is why I rejected the advice of the dietician, and why many other people do the same. She offered me an eating programme designed for the kind of energy balance that was appropriate for when I was slim, and did not take into account that a much smaller change would have been successful at first, as long as it gradually adapted itself as the programme continued. From the perspective of when I was very overweight, that was too big a jump for me to accept as something I was prepared to do, or even capable of doing at that time.

In the context of physical activity, the ratchet principle is widely used by trainers. Given someone who has not used their muscles much, it would be neither advisable nor safe for them to go on a five-mile run immediately, or start lifting heavy weights. Instead, they would do a little more than they have been used to doing, and when their body adapts to this, then we add more. This is a respectful way to treat the body, acknowledging that it will respond to you, but only at its own speed.

The ratcheting principle is an important topic throughout this book, both for the achievement phase and, perhaps more surprisingly, also for the maintenance phase. I would like to present an interesting way of thinking about it, and that is the concept of comfort zones.

Imagine a circle where all the things you are comfortable doing are inside that circle, and the more discomfort or effort that is required, the further away it is from the centre. We might call that circle your comfort zone, and here is how it might look:

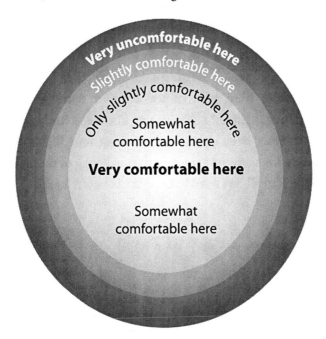

I used to do everything I could to stay right in the centre of my comfort zone, at least from an eating and activity point of view.

The interesting thing about comfort zones is that they are not fixed, and can change with time, especially as challenges are faced and overcome. In the context of the goals, the challenges we are facing are twofold. One is to increase our physical activity in a way that changes our body, and in particular stimulates the muscles to reduce their insulin resistance. The other is to modify the way we are eating.

As a simple example let's take climbing stairs for physical activity. At my former weight and level of exercise, climbing stairs was a long way out of my comfort zone. Similarly, reducing the calorie intake over time is another challenge, although in the next chapter it is suggested that not all calories are equal, and it is more important what you eat than just the number of calories. Still, for the sake of example, let us simply think of it for now as the number of calories a day.

Once you are prepared to spend some time in the 'slightly uncomfortable here' part of the comfort zone – for example climbing four flights of stairs – your brain and body will adapt to it. The comfort zone *grows*, and climbing four flights of stairs is now inside the comfort area, and the challenge of six flights is now where the four flights used to be. Here is how it looks:

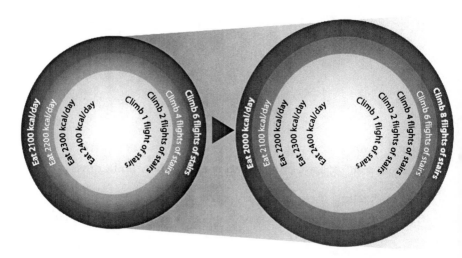

One final comment on ratcheting: after a while, it can become almost fun to go outside the comfort zone, knowing that at some level it will make a positive difference to your health and also to your whole life. This happened to me when I was in the maintenance phase and found I *enjoyed* being fit for its own sake, and started to really push the boundaries of what I could do. Although attaining this level is not really part of what I am recommending for success, it might be that once you start, you can begin to enjoy reaching out of your comfort zone, and be pleasantly surprised at how you develop in many different ways.

6 Nothing is forbidden

'Ah! You can't have *that!*'

I don't know about you, but there is something inside me that tends to rebel against that. I was in a French hospital bed when they discovered the high level of sugar in my blood. In the morning, they brought breakfast to the wards. In France it is common to have hot chocolate in the morning. I probably would not have cared too much whether I had chocolate or not, especially as it was coffee I used to drink. However, they told me I couldn't have the hot chocolate because I was diabetic. Apart from being a novel way to break the news to a patient, even to this day I still remember not being allowed to have hot chocolate.

Could this be another reason why people don't always succeed?

Oscar Wilde once said "The best way to resist temptation is to yield to it." So I decided from the beginning that nothing was forbidden, and I would never tell myself that there were things I couldn't have. I would not accept anyone else telling me either.

How can 'Nothing is forbidden' work in the long term?

It can work well if some of the above strategies are put into place. Let us use chocolate cake as our working example, and review the choices that have been outlined, in the order of the above sections.

Firstly, I could decide that in the long term it would not be good for me. Although I would *like* it, I did not really *want* it. Isn't it interesting how many times in life 'like' and 'want' are not the same thing? When this happens, I gently smile at it, acknowledge its presence and then build that decision in as a resource for future times.

Or I decide that I will have it, knowing it would only be a blip on the path to success, and that as long as I did not do it every time, this would be acceptable to me.

Secondly, I could have got into a habit where, without thinking, it does not attract me like it used to; or developed the habit of cutting a small piece from an already-existing piece; or choosing the smallest piece, whereas in former days I would have undoubtedly gone for the largest.

Thirdly, I could ask myself what kind of hunger I was experiencing, and how I would feel an hour or two after I had eaten it. Then either make a decision at that point, or go on to the next question.

Fourthly, I could ask myself what I would like to do instead of eating the chocolate cake, and if for example at a buffet, swap it out for something else. If being bored or restless is behind the desire to eat the cake, another choice is to engage in some interesting activity, and these are worth cultivating as part of the lifestyle change.

Or I could see it as an opportunity to ratchet down. Depending where I was in the process, I could choose to take a slightly smaller slice than I would normally have taken, putting it in the context of the direction my life would be taking.

Finally, as will be discussed in the next chapter, knowledge of why some foods are bad for you and how good food makes both a short- and long-term difference to your life is also a useful background to help you to freely and openly make a decision you are happy with.

Very recently I was at a birthday party where my daughter had made a very nice chocolate cake. I chose to take the slice I was offered, and enjoyed eating it with family and friends. There was some cake left over, and it sat in my house for a few days. It did not attract me, and I did not need self-control to keep away from it like I would have had in the past. I also know I could have watched it being thrown away without having those obsessive impulses to retrieve it like I used to have.

At no point along the way did I impose on myself any kind of injunction that I would be guilty of a crime if I had some chocolate cake, and this balance of freedom and responsibility means the whole situation can be approached in a positive way, which can eventually lead to taking the right decisions automatically.

7 Take it slowly and steadily

Once you seriously start a new lifestyle with the aim to get and stay fit for life, it is tempting to want to get it over with, and maybe do some unhelpful things in an attempt to speed it all up.

In some ways, this is like thinking of it as a running event. A crash diet is like a sprint. Sprinters can go very fast for a very short while, but cannot keep that speed up for a long distance. This lifetime programme is more like a marathon. Marathon runners pace themselves. They start, and continue, running more slowly than a sprinter, but the difference is that they keep on going. No marathon runner would start with an all-out sprint. Remember, it is a lifetime journey, and you will want to be able to keep going even when you have reached your target.

Something I encounter quite often is people who skip meals in an effort to reduce their weight more quickly. After all, if you only eat twice, or maybe even only once a day, it is easier to eat less, isn't it? If only it were that simple.

Let us look at this from an insulin point of view. If you have three meals a day, your blood sugar will go up whatever you eat. Insulin will be secreted to deal with it three times a day, and as long as the meals are relatively healthy, the food will be digested properly, with most of the sugar stored in the muscles and liver, and any excess stored as fat.

If you have three smaller meals a day with snacks in between, this may be even better from an insulin point of view. Indeed, I often split my lunch into two, or sometimes even three, sessions spread throughout the day. In addition I have never, under any circumstances, skipped breakfast.

Now, if there are only one or two meals a day, there will be larger insulin spikes, and more of the food will be turned into fat. Also, the body may think it is facing starvation, especially if it is breakfast that is missed out. There is then a gap of maybe 15-18 hours without food, and this may trigger it into further enhancing its ability to store fat, to reduce its metabolic rate and also to burn up muscle tissue for energy. This is a totally counterproductive state to get into.

Sometimes, there may be a medical case to shock the body for a short period, especially if the insulin resistance and blood sugar are at dangerous levels. This is often done by a period of medically-observed, extremely low-calorie intake. I would not for a moment want to discourage life-saving interventions.

However, even in this case the person has a lifetime ahead of them, and it is useful to think through the transition from this kind of therapy back to a normal lifestyle that will maintain the gains made for life.

If you want to adopt most of the ideas in this book, and still do a quick short sharp shock, this is OK and there is nothing wrong with this if you need a quick weight loss, or even better to start off a quick blood sugar reduction. What I would suggest in this case is simply to think through, or even better pre-rehearse, the transition to whatever lifestyle you would like to live by once the programme is over.

Otherwise, taking it slowly and steadily, reducing by one pound a week, or maybe at most two, and slowly ramping up the level of activity, may be the best option. This way, you are most likely to lose fat instead of muscle, let your skin follow the changes of your body size more easily, and allow the body to adjust its metabolism without giving any kind of starvation response. This will maximise the likelihood of achieving long-term success.

8   Be gentle with yourself, giving rewards often

It is great to feel and share the sense of achievement when you hit any mini-goals you have set yourself along the way. This can be highly motivating, and it is nice to reward yourself, or share the celebration with people close to you. The reward can of course be some of the food that you have been careful with, or even better it can be something you like doing and have promised yourself to wait until the target is met. Or maybe treat yourself to a massage. There are lots of opportunities to feel good about yourself along the way.

Sometimes the reward can come from outside, especially if you have supporters who are keen to see you succeed and celebrate with you, or if you are in a group where you all support each other.

Sometimes it can come from the inside, where the sheer satisfaction of achieving each stage is a reward in itself.

But what happens if you set a target and don't achieve it when you thought you would? This is a good time to think how a good friend and supporter would react if you told them. The chances are they would be very gentle and understanding, and if they understood the long-term goal would reassure you that this was just a blip along the way. So, why not treat yourself as such a supportive friend?

Indeed, it might be useful to pre-rehearse this even before it happens. Imagine that along the way your weight stays static for a few weeks or increases slightly. Now, being very relaxed when you imagine it, how supportive can you be to yourself, in a way that will help keep you on track?

Along the way, I hit a plateau and my weight was relatively constant for about three weeks. This was a frustrating time. However, I knew I was doing the right things, and gently told myself that my body was simply making adjustments, and as long as I continued progressing in the right direction, it would be OK in the long term. There are times when I am not always so gentle with myself, but in this context it is quite important.

Another area where being gentle with yourself can help is in handling stress. We all need a little challenge in our lives in order to grow and develop, but when it gets out of hand it can be a destructive force. And sometimes the outside world seems to demand so much. A useful way to think about stress is that it occurs when the perceived demands on you are greater than what you think your ability is to meet those demands. There are various strategies that might help. One might be to stop and ask "What would actually happen if I chose not to meet that demand?" especially if it is a demand placed on yourself. Another option is to actually apply the above definition of stress. If you have already built some stress distinctions as outlined in the earlier section, it is useful to review each different type of stress from the above definition, and look to see to what extent it is really coming from inside you. In either case, it may be useful to imagine discussing it with the kind of supportive friend mentioned above.

There is another not so obvious reason why this is important. Being under stress causes other hormones to be released. These stress hormones, such as cortisol, actually reduce insulin and increase blood sugar, as does a lack of sufficient sleep.

9   Make sure you like the new you

Earlier, the man who had lost an incredible amount of weight was mentioned. He became arrogant, promiscuous and selfish, and neither he nor his wife liked or respected the kind of person he had become. After a while, he put the weight back on. We don't know exactly why all his work and success was reversed, but if you did not like or respect the person you had become, what motivation is there to continue?

If you make a transformation that changes your physical appearance, have more energy, and exude more health and confidence, this is bound to change your sense of identity at some level. It can also change how you connect and interact with family, friends and other people in general, and how they connect with you. It would be really good if all of this were totally positive.

So, how will you relate to yourself as you continue through the programme, and also when you get into the maintenance phase? What kind of person do you want to become? This is an ideal opportunity to consider some kind of change. Perhaps to decide whether you want to be an inspiration to others, or a better example to your family, do something ambitious or outrageous, or simply continue exactly as you were except in a more healthy way. What is important here is that you like and respect the person you will become, and the more this happens, the more likely you are to keep going.

Also important is how you relate to others, and what kind of support and encouragement they give you. If you treat others with respect, you can easily gain their support and encouragement.

It is a good precaution to think in advance how you would want to face any of the different kinds of discouragement you might encounter. It may be that the change can destabilise a relationship if it is not handled with sensitivity; or it may even be threatening to colleagues, especially in a competitive social or work environment. The kind of change this programme can give in terms of physical appearance, strength and energy can help make you more influential, get listened to more and taken more seriously. It may be unfair, but people are people, and I have seen this happen. Your friends and supporters may love this change, but don't be surprised if a very small minority does not share in this, and even tries to trip you up along the way. If you recognise this, and smilingly and gently treat it as nothing more than yet another sign of your success, it may eventually dissolve it. Even if it doesn't, you might find yourself able to generate even more desire to succeed and show those people what you are now capable of.

How you treat your significant others is also very important. There was a televised programme where a man who was very overweight went to a weight-losing event, and had made a good start in terms of how much he had reduced. He went back to his wife and children, stormed into the house, flung open the fridge door, and started throwing things out. "We won't have this! We can't have that! This is going!" he bellowed. It is interesting to speculate what kind of messages he was giving his family, and what kind of long-term support he would get – especially in the way he was imposing on them in a sudden, forceful and totally unsympathetic way. Maybe he was unwittingly sowing the seeds of rebellion, or even sabotage. If he also treated himself that way, it would be interesting to know whether he lasted the course, and managed to maintain it if he did.

This is where the decision to succeed even when there are distractions all around is crucial. I wanted to change to a much more healthy way of eating, and some of my family didn't. We handled this with ease and mutual respect. We agreed to have in the house my milk and their milk, my spread and their butter, my muesli-based breakfast cereal and their more sugary choices. We had, and still have, chocolate and biscuits in the house, and I took responsibility to make whatever eating choices I wanted. There was no undue pressure for anyone to change. Over time, many (but not all) of these distinctions have melted away, usually towards the healthier choices.

With some thought, it can be integrated into social situations. If you are in a group of people where each takes a turn to buy a round of drinks, this can result in drinking a lot more beer or other alcoholic drinks than you might actually want. You can choose to stop going to such groups, but if you like that kind of social interaction, such avoidance does not confront the issue. Instead, you could decide how much you are prepared to drink, and for the other rounds, simply and without fuss buy something like sparkling water. Note that pure orange juice or other popular pub fruit drinks have a far higher calorie count and a much higher tendency to put sugar in the bloodstream than beer, so it is worth being careful about swapping to a large quantity of these. Or if it is a coffee-drinking group, note that a modern-day latte with high amounts of sugar and fat can be very destructive to your programme, and yet a simple change to, say, an unsugared black coffee is unlikely to upset the social interaction. Remember, 'simple' does not necessarily mean 'easy' and it might take a change of habit to achieve this, but it is this very kind of change that will underpin your success. It is surprising how quickly this behaviour change can become accepted. The ratchet philosophy could be applied here very nicely to help make this happen more smoothly.

In this way, one can run the programme with genuine help and support, and yet in a way that respects both yourself and others. This is a part of liking the kind of person you become as a result of the changes, and minimises both self-induced or external rebellion against your programme.

A somewhat subtle but very important part of liking and respecting the person you will become, and indeed who you are throughout the journey, is how you choose to label yourself. This can significantly affect how much you will like, and are driven towards becoming, the new you.

A label tends to be a noun or adjective applied to you as a person, either by people around you or even by yourself. Labels tend to make generalised statements about the kind of person you are across all contexts of your life, and are often very unhelpful. For example: greedy, undeserving, control freak, unlucky, victim, shy or addict to name but a few. An extreme example of how the same behaviour is regarded totally differently as a result of labelling is to consider the difference between 'freedom fighter' and 'terrorist' and how it changes or even reverses how you feel about the person being described.

There is a sense of freedom in deciding which labels you want and which you don't. One way to challenge a label is either to reframe it, or turn it into a verb perhaps modified by a 'not yet'.

One example is the label 'I am a food addict'. From this perspective, it is difficult to consider succeeding at anything to do with losing weight, and the label builds in defeat before you start. A realistic way to restate this might be 'I sometimes get strong impulses to eat, and have not yet learned to overcome them'. This at least unfreezes the description and opens a path forward.

Another is 'I am a victim, and what has happened to me is purely genetic'. No-one should deny the effect of genetic background, and confronting or denying it directly is never going to succeed, especially as there is usually some truth behind it. It might be interesting for people where one or both parents have had Type 2 diabetes to reflect on how much might be due to genes, and how much might be due to inherited lifestyle and habits. It is likely that both nature and nurture have had an influence. One possible way to empower yourself might be 'Even though I have a genetic bias, my lifestyle has contributed to this, and there is still something I can do about it'. There are of course many other appropriate ways of doing this, depending on the way you would like to think about things like this. For the first couple of days after my diagnosis of diabetes, I regarded myself as a victim. I only really started taking action once I shed the self-imposed label and accepted my own responsibility for my plight.

Another is 'I am the kind of person who does not deserve to succeed'. There may be many ways forward from here. An interesting one might be to take the deserving and put it into something bigger than just the one person. Simply by succeeding, you can become a shining example to others, such as immediate members of your family or community, and by force of example inspire people around you, perhaps to succeed themselves. All these other people deserve for you to succeed, don't they? Once you recognise that a label is in place, there are many ways to counter its effect, or even turn it into a positive label.

I would like to finish this section with two of my own examples of where self-labelling can be powerful.

The first is simply choosing a different or opposite label. Before I started my journey, I labelled myself as old. As a direct result, I missed out on recognising the clear symptoms of diabetes. Also, later in the journey, I argued that I was too old to start doing certain activities. Over ten years later, I think of myself as young, and open to new ideas and activities. This very positively affects the whole way I think about myself.

The second one is the exact reversal of the 'food addict' process above. I was of course labelled as being a diabetic, which I accepted at first. But when I started to reduce my blood sugar below the diabetic threshold, I was referred to as 'a diabetic who was controlling it with diet and exercise'. Apart from rejecting the word diet in favour of lifestyle change, this was absolutely not how I wanted to regard myself. So I redefined it as 'My pancreas is healthy enough. I was simply out of balance, and am now restoring that balance'. Soon after that, I froze it back into a label I still adopt today with pleasure every time I use it, and that is 'ex-diabetic'. At first, I got a lot of negative feedback, especially from some members of the medical community, who had been trained with the Universal Truth that once you cross that threshold, you are a diabetic for life. They certainly did not like it when my label challenged that. But it is a label I now carry with pride, especially as I recently got medical confirmation of this, as will be described at the very end of this book.

10 Embrace all experiences to build your resources

Up to now, and certainly since starting the programme, you will have had a lot of experiences. Some of them you may have labelled as good, and some may be labelled as bad. And yet, both are part of you.

Good experiences can help motivate you and continue to help pull you through. The time your blood sugar was lower than you expected, or you broke through a certain weight, or were able to buy the next clothes size down. Or maybe do something physical that you had formerly thought would be impossible for you.

These experiences are natural to use as ways to help reach success. But what about experiences where things did not go as well as you had hoped? Or had lapsed or stumbled in a way that you were not proud of?

Let me give a couple of examples, just to illustrate how one could think about such experiences in a different way, and also use them as resources to help you.

The first one happened to me at an airport, while I was waiting for the gate to open. There was someone giving out free Belgian chocolates, and as I walked past, she asked me if I wanted one. I initially hesitated, but took one anyway and ate it. Then she asked if I wanted a second one. At this point I thanked her, but told her

I really didn't want to eat two chocolates. However, she was very persuasive, so I took the second one too. I had already started to get into the habit of eating fewer sweet foods, and after a few minutes I started to feel just a little sick. At this point, it would have been easy to recriminate myself for being so gullible and stupid, and I almost did. Then I stopped, smiled, and thought 'Good! This is how I *want* to feel if I eat chocolates when I really didn't want them.'

I feel quite sure that this experience, looked at in this way, has helped me feel less attracted to chocolates. Although I still sometimes eat one if I want to, I never allow myself to be persuaded to eat one if I don't really want it.

A similar reaction helped me recognise when I had successfully built in a habit. I was on a long escalator, and at this stage I would run up to the top. Note that when I first started developing this as a habit I would walk up. As time went on, I reviewed the habit and decided from then on to run. In front of me was someone with a large piece of luggage, totally blocking my way forward. I felt a surge of resentment and frustration, and my impulse was to express this. Then I realised what I was doing, stopped, smiled, and thought 'Good! This is how I *want* to feel when I cannot run up the escalator. It proves that the habit is truly formed.'

There may be lots of past experiences to help in all kinds of different ways. For example, to answer the question "How will I feel in two hours if I eat this now?" Or perhaps to remember an energy crash or a bout of irritability following a junk food snack or breakfast. It is easy to brush these away as having been weak, or greedy, or whatever negative cast is natural to put on it. But now, it might be useful to relive these, and be able to have them right at your fingertips to help you make the decisions you want, almost without thinking.

Summary of mental tools

The above ideas are just that. Different people will prefer different sections. While I would encourage you to read and try out each section, and indeed to revisit this chapter a few times along the journey, feel free to pick and choose which of these you would like to work with.

I would just like to finish this chapter with two more points.

When faced with a long and slow path to success, it is tempting to wish there were a magic pill you could take to fix it all. There are of course medications for Type 2 diabetes, and it is important to take them if there is no other short-term way of lowering your blood sugar. There also exist some drugs to help lose weight. The most popular ones work either by inhibiting the absorption of fats from your digestive system into your body, or by reducing the appetite signals. Both have their place, and there are times when their use can be very appropriate. However, once these start being taken, one can get to rely on them, and in that case they tend to be a lifetime prescription. The more you can achieve without the use of such drugs, the more the success will be yours, and the healthier and more natural the result will be. I was surprised by what I could achieve by simply changing my thinking in the above ways, and it makes the success even more precious.

Finally, modern-day food and lifestyles can promote and encourage cravings for sugar and high-fat foods, often deliberately so. It is easy to think 'My body is telling me what to do. I listen to it, and do what it tells me.' Put this way, it is a very convincing argument to continue careering towards an overweight and diabetic future.

However, in the end, that is exactly the kind of thinking you want. You __do__ want to listen to your body, and do what it tells you. It is just a case of being sure that it is telling you the right things.

It is a bit like having a boss who is going in the wrong direction, and dragging you along with him. Your body might have become confused after extended periods of feeding and treating it in a way that it was not designed to cope with. Much of this programme is about re-educating and retraining your mind and body so that you can listen to it and do what it says, as a part of your future lifestyle. When this happens, your journey really is starting to become like paddling downstream.

CHAPTER FIVE

The achievement phase

This chapter is devoted to the more physical side of the equation, specifically eating and physical activity. There are some concepts branded as universal truths, and this chapter will show they are not at all universal, but nevertheless helpful guidelines as long as their limitations are understood. In fact, everything in this chapter is merely a guideline to use some of the ideas in the previous chapters to help you succeed.

My journey

Even as the ideas in the previous chapters were still forming, I started the process going. I decided to aim at an approximately equal balance of reducing my food intake and increasing my physical activity. As I was aiming at one to two pounds per week, this represents an average of about 250-500 kcal worth of extra activity every day, and also a similar amount of food reduction. Note that 250-500 kcal of energy is typically 30-60 minutes of reasonably vigorous activity if it is all done at once.

Another decision was not to be a calorie-counter all my life. Instead, the aim was to become calorie-aware, so that in the end I would almost instinctively know the right amounts. To achieve this, I started a phase of carefully looking at food labels, and was initially shocked by how much sugar is being added to almost everything I looked at, including yoghurts, well-known cereals, baked beans, most processed foods and even probiotic drinks marketed as being healthy. Then, for a period of only a few weeks, I kept a food diary, writing down everything I ate. Some people say food diaries are great as they make you aware of what you are eating, and this is certainly true. For me, the idea was simply part of the process to increase my awareness of what my food actually contained.

So while I was ratcheting down on the amount of food I was eating, and more importantly also starting to change the type of food, I turned my attention to activity. I hated the idea of exercise, as my school experiences had not left pleasant memories, and also running had been handed out to me as a punishment.

So following the earlier distinction I had made, I built up two different ways of achieving this amount of physical activity.

The first way was initially meant to be the main theme, and that was to make sure that, at every opportunity, I chose to move where I had previously remained still, and furthermore to embed this as a habit. So, every time I saw a lift, I would aim to take the stairs, and when I was on an escalator, I would walk to the top. At airports with a moving walkway, I would choose to walk, even with my baggage.

I also chose that when I walked anywhere, I would swap out my slow dawdle for a briskly paced walk. In principle, this does not add much to the amount of energy consumed during the walk, but it did raise my heart rate and caused my muscles to work at a higher pace, both of which are vital ingredients for starting to tackle insulin resistance and also other health issues.

After a while, the body accommodates itself to this, and I could ratchet up this part of the programme. Now I would run up escalators, and some of the longer ones were quite challenging and left me breathing quite hard at the end. When I went up stairs, I would try to match or exceed the speed of people walking up the escalator, and similarly for people walking along the moving walkway at airports. This helped to add to the fun of it, once I had got that little bit lighter and fitter. This was only a few months into the programme.

For the second part of doing the physical activity, I chose at least in the first instance to join a small local gym. I had no idea what to do, but was soon shown, and also given a programme that taught me about my body and also enabled me to see the progress I was making. I was asked to do an exercise, for instance at first walking on a treadmill at six kilometres per hour for four minutes, or going on the rowing machine at a particular resistance level for three minutes. After each exercise, I measured my heart rate and recorded it. When my heart rate started to become lower for the same amount of exercise, the exercise was increased – either by time, or by intensity or speed. As time went on, I was able to do more and more for the same amount of heart rate rise. I was becoming fitter, and as a direct result also increasingly able to burn more calories.

Similarly with the weight machines. At the beginning, I could only move light weights a few times in a row, and as time progressed, the weights could be set higher, or a higher number of repetitions could be done.

At this point, my weight was decreasing by around six to seven pounds a month, but due to the exercise I was doing, I was toning up my muscles and increasing their mass, so I was actually losing more fat than the weight loss was indicating. My morning blood sugar levels were decreasing too. My doctor had wanted me to aim at reducing my sugar levels to 13 mmol/l (240 mg/dl) within three months, and in fact it fell faster than that. So he then suggested I aim for 8 mmol/l (144 mg/dl) if I possibly could.

I remember one event at the gym that made me realise how far I had progressed. I used to go to a class where we all had steps, and to music we would get on and off the step, sometimes raising knees. There were only two kinds of steps: low ones and high ones. I was a beginner, so I used to get to the class early to take a small step. One day I got there and all the small steps were taken, and all that was left were the higher steps. I was angry, and unhappily took the step to start the class. As the class progressed, I realised that this was now the right level for me, and my frustration turned to satisfaction. From that day on, I stopped going to the beginners' class, and moved to the intermediate and advanced classes. Me! Who had always hated and avoided exercise. I was almost beginning to enjoy it now.

It was not too long after that when my fasting blood sugar dropped below 8 mmol/l (144 mg/dl), and to my amazement continued to fall. Eventually it fell to around 5 mmol/l (90 mg/dl) which is what would be expected for normal healthy people, and certainly even below what would be expected for prediabetes.

All of this happened around the time I had lost 10-15% of my weight, and was just under halfway towards my weight-loss target. There was now no question of going on to any medication, and from a diabetic point of view I had fully achieved the blood sugar level target.

Looking back, the rest of that first 15 month period seemed uneventful in retrospect, except perhaps that I remained being a gym user, and moved from the safe environment of a small gym to a larger more impersonal gym. I suspect I would not have got the help, support and education there that I got in the crucial early days of the smaller gym.

Having set up new habits, new distinctions, better eating habits, and doing a reasonable amount of exercise, I simply continued. There were some celebration points: when I broke through 100 kilograms; when I had to change all my clothes to a smaller size; when I had to change my clothes a second time. There was also a plateau when my weight did not move for three to four weeks, and my attitude to that was that my body was adjusting itself before moving to the next level. Just to make sure I wasn't somehow kidding myself, this was the only period where I kept a food diary for a few weeks. At the end of 15 months, I got to the kind of shape and the kind of weight that I had always wanted. My total weight loss was almost 40 kilograms. The pictures below show the difference between when I started and 15 months later.

There were some other changes, which are apparently to be expected. My blood pressure decreased, and my cholesterol levels became good. Indeed, every one of the criteria for metabolic syndrome mentioned in an earlier chapter became within healthy limits. In addition, I was becoming much more alert, had higher energy and was able to overcome challenges at work which probably would have defeated me before. For a while, I found it hard to believe my side view, and I admit I used to stop by reflective shop windows and gaze quite admiringly at the reflection. After a year or so, this passed too, as I totally accepted my new appearance.

Interestingly, this all came with a number of unexpected changes, some of which were very positive, and some slightly less so.

The first one was that I have a network of friends and acquaintances that I sometimes see only once a year, or even less often. For these people, the transformation looked lightning-fast, even though at the time it felt slow to me. Almost every one of my friends, and also relatives, did not recognise me when they saw me. For a couple of years, it was always at the forefront of my mind when I met an old acquaintance or colleague 'Is this the first time they have seen me since I reached my target?' And I learned to introduce myself to these people. I did meet someone who was very shocked to see me as she knew someone who had lost weight because they were very ill, and I could assure her I was healthier than ever before. After a while this settled down, although even seven years later I arranged to meet a former colleague at a conference, and she had asked for me at the desk saying, "I want to meet Barry. Have you seen him? He is, well... quite big." Each time this happened, I accepted it with an attitude of enjoying it, taking it as another sign of my success, and reinforcing the wish never to go back.

The second one was that I used to get too hot very quickly. I had always been happy with cold weather and hated summer, even when I lived in Canada for a couple of years. Now this had reversed itself, and I discovered it the hard way. I did some outdoor activities one March and dressed lightly, as I had always done before. It was sunny, and by my former standards, not cold. However, I found the temperature so uncomfortable that all the enjoyment was gone. Sometimes in the School of Life, if you don't learn a lesson the first time round, it continues to repeat until you do learn it. This happened to me three times before I realised that my response to temperature was forever changed. This is one effect I did not anticipate in advance.

My former self sweated a lot, and with this changed response to temperature, this went away. Nowadays I still sweat when I do intensive exercise, but no longer on a normal day-to-day basis.

One amusing change was that my tolerance to alcoholic drinks was reduced. Before, I could and would drink and not feel it, but now find it easy to get light-headed after a much smaller amount. This makes it quite natural to drink a lot less, and I happily think of it as one of the many ways this programme has helped save money.

Snoring while asleep also totally stopped.

Perhaps the most unexpected, unplanned and yet very significant change was one that happened a little more slowly, and continued happening during the first year after achieving my target weight. It also helped change the way I think about what we are doing to our bodies.

I suffered from a skin disease called psoriasis, which is a condition where the skin dries out and gets covered with white flakes, and can crack and itch in a very uncomfortable way. I was quite unhappy to be in someone's car as I often left visible flakes on the carpeting over a long journey. With my former way of thinking, there was surely nothing I was doing to cause this, as both my mother and one of my sisters had it even worse than I did. However, it did get worse during a certain stressful period of my life. I had been through a phase of taking medication in an attempt to get rid of it, but nothing had worked. So it was clearly a genetic disease, and I was stuck with it. Or so I thought.

Within the first year, the itching had abated, and the affected areas were shrinking. After about another year, there was no more psoriasis. Since then, it has never come back.

This is not necessarily saying that embarking on such a programme is a cure for skin disease. However, with modern-day eating habits, we put a lot of unhealthy things into our bodies, many of which the body does not know what to do with. Such habits do not always supply all the nutrients or even the pure water it needs to maintain it in tip-top condition, and this can be linked to many modern-day symptoms and illnesses. All I know is that my psoriasis totally disappeared without me trying to do anything specific to make it happen. I am convinced that even if I had a genetic propensity for psoriasis, my former lifestyle aggravated the condition enough to make my skin break out the way it did. This slowly reversed itself when my body was given a chance to get back to its more natural balance. I am also convinced that this is only one of the many benefits that can result from such a lifestyle change.

Towards the end of the achievement phase, I made one last visit to the hospital dietician whom I had met right at the very beginning of the journey. This appointment had been booked a year in advance. She was delighted to see me, and I think perhaps a little surprised. At the end of the interview, she unexpectedly said to me, "We are seeing a very low success rate indeed, and would like to know how you achieved this so that we can better help other people." I was somewhat saddened by this and wanted, and still want, to help people like this in some way. I gave her an early copy of this book, which I was drafting even then to help me capture, describe and organise the methods and processes I was using. I hope it helped make a difference.

As I was approaching the end of the achievement phase, the maintenance phase was right in front of me. I had known that sooner or later it would come, and had prepared as much as I could for it. Some of the mental preparation included the development of habits intentionally chosen to support this phase. However, life is full of surprises, and I certainly did not predict how the maintenance phase was going to work out for me.

Are you at risk?

There are many different ways to judge whether you are at risk of diseases in general, ranging from genetic analysis, ethnicity, blood pressure, sugar and cholesterol measurements, body geometry and a host of others.

For simplicity, I would like to describe the simplest ways of doing this at home, without needing any analytic equipment. Note that these are only a guideline, and are not rigidly correct in all circumstances.

The first is a measurement called Body Mass Index, or BMI for short. It is simply your weight in kilograms, divided by the square of your height in metres. So, as an example, someone weighing 92 kg who is 185 cm tall has a BMI of 92 / (1.85 x 1.85), which is about 26.9.

BMI started life as nothing more than mathematicians trying to model human parameters. Then in 1985 there was an initial attempt to use BMI to categorise people as underweight, normal or overweight. The numbers were different for men and women, as they were based on the overweight statistics available at that time. So, the overweight limit for males was a BMI of 27.8, and for females it was 27.3.

A little later, it was changed to become the BMI limits that are used today. The numbers were simplified, and the gender difference swept away. The range 18.5-25 is considered normal, less than 18.5 underweight, and from 25 onwards considered overweight. A fourth category was added for people with a BMI of 30 and higher, and called obese, and further categories added at 35 and 40 to represent different shades of obese.

So with a flourish of the pen, a huge number of people were suddenly categorised as overweight. Consider the poor 92 kg person with a BMI of 26.9. He, like millions of others, would have been labelled as normal, and suddenly the guideline changed and they would now be categorised as overweight.

Then the risk of contracting Type 2 diabetes became tied to the overweight and obese categories, as shown in the graph:

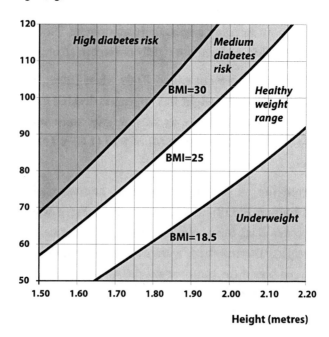

There are some other traps when simply using BMI as the only guideline. It does not take account of the state of your muscles. One of my friends was a bodybuilder, and he had almost no fat on him at all. However, he had very large muscles, and his Body Mass Index was well into the thirties. As a result he was quoted double premiums on his insurance because they thought he was obese, and it was quite a fight to reverse it. This is a totally incorrect misuse of BMI!

However, if you are sedentary and don't have well-developed bulging muscles, BMI is already a reasonably good guideline.

There are a couple of other easy measurements which are helpful in approaching this. The first is a simple measurement of the circumference of your waist, and the associated health risks are shown below:

Waist Measurement (Males)	Waist Measurement (Females)	Health risk
94 cm *(37 inches)*	80 cm *(32 inches)*	Moderate
102 cm *(40 inches)*	88 cm *(35 inches)*	High

The second easy measurement takes into account that extra fat around the waist gives a far greater health risk than the same amount of fat around the buttocks and thighs. Indeed, there is evidence that fat around the waist is the result of high insulin levels, so this is even more significant for predicting Type 2 diabetes. There is a growing opinion that the ratio of waist to hip measurement is the most indicative of true risk, even over BMI and waist circumference.

Waist -Hip ratio (Males)	Waist - Hip ratio (Females)	Health risk
0.9	0.75	Moderate
1.0	0.80	High

So the question is how do you know you are at risk, and what is your ideal weight? If your BMI is over 25 and if your waist circumference or waist-hip ratio is in the moderate category, you might be standing on the threshold of a heightened risk, whether now or in 10-15 years' time.

If you are of Afro-Caribbean or South Asian origin, this appears to raise the risk of contracting Type 2 diabetes compared to a European or white American of the same weight. This is also true for some native American tribes. In this case, it may be wise to regard the values in the above tables as a little too lax, and maybe aim for a BMI of around 23, and perhaps also to regard the high-risk waist circumference as 10 cm lower than in the table above, and act accordingly.

If your BMI is 30 or over, and you are in the high-risk category, it is really very wise indeed to start a programme such as the one described in this book. I left it almost too late, and hope that others can make better choices than I did at the time.

So what is your ideal weight? What numbers might be put into your initial mission statement? If your BMI is into the thirties or higher, it may make sense to aim at something like 25-26 to start with, or perhaps even slightly higher, subject to your circumference and ratio measurements fitting in. If you are already have Type 2 diabetes and a high level of blood sugar, reaching this kind of BMI should already have a very beneficial effect on lowering these levels. Many people in the early stages of Type 2 diabetes find their blood sugar levels return to normal after a 10-15% weight reduction.

A BMI much lower than 25 might be difficult to achieve, and it could be very tempting to want to get skinnier and skinnier. For a while I almost got pulled into that potentially dangerous area.

As you start getting closer to the target, it is a good idea to check it out and decide what end result you would really want, which is easier once you are closer to it and have success and momentum working for you.

What are calories?

When it comes to dealing with the contribution of being overweight to Type 2 diabetes, or simply in the context of losing weight, the word 'calorie' is nearly always used. So this section will focus on what a calorie actually is, and how many we actually need.

A calorie as originally defined by scientists is simply a unit of energy, and quite a small one too. It is the energy required to heat one gram of water by one degree Celsius. There is a similar unit called a Joule, which although being the correct unit for scientific use, has simply not managed to replace the calorie when it comes to describing food. One calorie is about 4.2 Joules.

When we talk about 'one calorie' in food, what we actually mean is 1,000 scientific calories. Sometimes the word has a capital C to indicate it is a bigger unit, so that we really mean Calories. To avoid the confusion such a system can cause, the term 'kcal' (kilocalories, still often referred to as calories) will be used from now on in the book for any quantitative description. Just to make it clear, a slice of bread containing 100 kcal (usually in speech referred to as 100 calories) is actually 100,000 scientific calories. This slice of bread would provide the body with an amount of energy equivalent to that used to take a whole litre of water at ice temperature and bring it to the boil. Food labels often show the number of kcal in a given size serving, usually but not always for 100g, and often also give the energy in kilojoules as well. So you might see for the slice of bread '100 kcal, 418 kJ'.

Where does this energy go? Some of it goes into body maintenance and repair, breathing and digestion, and also to run the brain and the nervous system. For example, the brain typically uses 400 kcal/day. Some of it goes on physical activity. Any left over gets stored as fat.

Let us take our 100g slice of bread and see how much activity it can fuel. A person weighing 80 kg would typically use 100 kcal in walking a mile at a moderate to brisk pace. A heavier person would use more calories, and a lighter person would use fewer. So a large latte and muffin as served in some coffee shops could provide enough fuel to walk about eight miles. Or to put it another way, if you wanted to walk off the effects of such a snack, be prepared to walk about eight miles.

There are some statements made as if they were universal truths about balancing calories. They say that if the calories you eat are more than the calories you use, you will gain weight. If they are the same, you stay the same, and if they are fewer, you lose weight. It is often quoted as a mathematical truth. Try telling that to some of my colleagues who are skinny and desperate to gain weight!

I would like to suggest that the body's metabolism is far more complex than that. 'Calories in' is easy – that is simply what you eat and drink. However, the body has some intricate balancing mechanisms, and 'Calories out' is nothing like as obvious. For example, the average person eats about 25 tons of food in their lifetime. Most adults do not vary their weight by more than 25 kg. If weight management were just energy in versus energy out, to keep within 25 kg means we would need to accurately fine-tune what we eat to within one part in a thousand. Even the most obsessive dieter cannot possibly do that. Even when my eating got out of control, I did not vary by more than 50 kg, which is less than one part in 500 of my lifetime intake.

Note that not all calories are equal, especially when taken from an insulin point of view. The effect of eating depends on many factors, such as the nature of the food itself, how quickly it releases glucose into the bloodstream, the time of day it is eaten, how relaxed or stressed you are when you eat, and how far apart one intake is from another. It is worth remembering that a high level of insulin primes the body to store and retain fat.

Perhaps we can learn from people who intentionally put on a lot of weight, an extreme example being the Japanese Sumo wrestlers. They certainly eat a lot of food – up to 20,000 kcal/day, some of it protein and much of it white rice which quickly releases sugar, and also drink beer with it. What they do to ensure the weight is piled on is also instructive. An important part of their weight gain is that they skip breakfast, and do heavy exercise for up to five hours to bring on a starvation response. Then they have a huge lunch, and go to sleep immediately afterwards. Sleep is a time of low metabolism, so the insulin level rises sharply and the excess food is converted to fat. Later in the day, they have another large meal, and again immediately sleep afterwards, through the night. This cycle of eating only two meals a day and then sleeping right afterwards is a good one to avoid if you wish to be successful.

Having said all this, if you are overweight and sedentary, then aiming to reduce the calories in and increase calories out is a reasonably good guideline. You can act **as if** it is true that when you eat more than you use, you will gain weight, and if you eat less than you use, your weight will start to reduce.

So how many calories a day do we need? This again is complex, and depends on age, gender, build, weight, height and level of physical activity. A quantity called the Base Metabolic Rate (BMR) has been defined, which is the energy you would use if you did absolutely no physical activity at all. We then multiply the BMR by a factor depending on how active you are to get an idea of the number of kcal/day you need. This is of course only a guideline and not a rule, and for example people with a very muscular build will probably need more kcal/day than the BMR estimates give. However some interesting ideas and results come out of this kind of calculation.

One way to get an overview is to look at the following two graphs. Here is one for males:

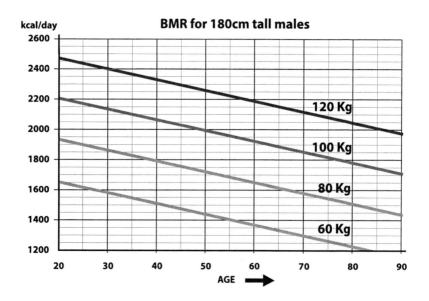

Here is one for females:

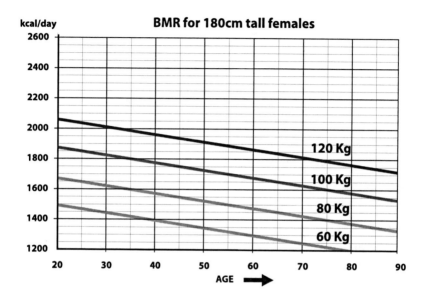

BMR for 180cm tall females

kcal/day

120 Kg
100 Kg
80 Kg
60 Kg

AGE ➡

If you wish to use these graphs, look up the BMR for your age and weight. For males, add 5 kcal/day for every centimetre you are over 180 cm, or subtract 5 kcal/day for every centimetre you are below 180 cm. For females, add 2 kcal/day for every centimetre you are over 180 cm, or subtract 2 kcal/day for every centimetre you are below 180 cm. If you prefer to calculate these for yourself, the explicit formulae are given in Appendix 4.

Once you have the Base Metabolic Rate, to get a rough idea of the number of calories a day you need, multiply the number by:

1.2	if you do just a little exercise, but sit around most of the day
1.375	if you do light exercise one to three times a week
1.55	if you do moderate exercise three to five times a week
1.725	if you do hard exercise six to seven times a week
1.9	if you do very hard exercise, exercise twice a day or do a very physically demanding job

As an example, let us take a 70-year-old man who is 180 cm tall, weighs 80 kg and is only lightly active. Perhaps that is a walk every day and doing some gardening or housework. Looking at the graph, the Base Metabolic Rate is 1,600 kcal/day, and with an activity factor of 1.375, would typically require 2,200 kcal a day. The same man, doing the same activity, would have needed almost 2,500 kcal/day more when he was 40.

The definitions of the labels of lightly active, moderately active, or heavily active are slightly vague, so this is at best nothing more than a rough guideline. Take the case of someone who sits at a desk eight hours a day, then goes to the gym and does moderate exercise. They may very well be less active in total than someone who works long hours on their feet all day, such as a supermarket shelf stacker or a nurse in an emergency ward. However, the graphs do show some interesting things.

▶ Men seem to require more calories than women even of the same height and weight, even if their levels of activity are comparable

▶ As you lose weight, you will need fewer calories even if you maintain your current level of physical activity

▶ As you get older, you will need fewer calories even if you maintain your current level of physical activity

▶ As men get older, their calorie requirement tends to reduce more quickly than for women

In particular, if you go from say 120 kg to 80 kg, not only does your calorie requirement become a lot lower, but in addition the same amount of exercise (e.g. walking a mile) uses far fewer calories too. These are worth knowing in advance, as they can help you understand why the need to ratchet all the way to achievement, and even through maintenance, will always be present.

As you start such a programme, especially if it involves a significant weight loss, you will be aiming to create an imbalance between calories in and calories out. So let us look at how it relates to weight, and reduction of body fat. Each pound of fat represents 3,500 kcal, and each kilogram is just over 7,500 kcal. So to reduce by one pound per week requires a reduction of 3,500 kcal, or 500 kcal each and every day.

Imagine a programme that aims to reduce weight by six pounds a month that is based on eating changes alone, and that there is no change in physical activity. This is what many dieters commonly do, and some strive to reduce even more quickly. This would mean reducing your food intake by 750 kcal/day. This is a significant reduction for a reasonably modest weight loss rate, which would have to be maintained every day. If this is done by simple calorie restriction, great care would need to be taken to ensure that the body still gets all the nutrients it needs. This is only one of the reasons that physical activity is best considered as an integral part of such a programme.

Nutrients in our food

In order to make the best choices, it is useful to understand a little about the nutrients in our food. The more you know, the better, and if you want to ensure the right kind of health for you –whether it be to maintain your brain, your bones, or antioxidants – there is a lot of specialist knowledge available and a lot more to learn.

Even though a good knowledge of nutrition is important, I would like to present a simplified overview of the different food types, and some guidelines on how you might succeed without needing detailed knowledge. If you follow the general direction described below, you will be taking some significant steps in the right direction anyway.

The easiest way to know more about what you are eating, especially if you are buying packaged food at supermarkets, is to look at the food label. There are many different kinds of food labelling, and here are two instructive examples:

Label 1 – *a cereal biscuit*

Label 2 – *steamed salmon*

NUTRITION: *Typical Average Values*

	Per biscuit	Per 100g
Energy	284 kJ/ 67 kcal	1516 kJ/ 358 kcal
Protein	2.2g	11.5g
Carbohydrate	12.9g	68.6g
(of which sugars	0.8g	4.4g)
Fat	0.4g	2.0g
(of which saturates	0.1g	0.6g)
Fibre	1.9g	10.0g
Sodium	0.05g	0.26g
Salt	0.12g	0.65g
Vitamins and iron		
Thiamin (B1)	0.2mg	0.9mg
Riboflavin (B2)	0.2mg	1.2mg
Niacin	2.6mg	13.6mg
Folic acid	32.0µg	170.0µg
Iron	2.5mg	11.9mg

One biscuit provides 16% of the Recommended Daily Allowance (RDA) of the vitamins & iron listed.

100g provides 85% of the RDA of the vitamins and minerals listed

NUTRITION:

Typical values	Per 100g
Energy kJ	745
Energy kcal	180
Protein	23.5g
Carbohydrate	0.2g
of which sugars	0.2g
Fat	9.3g
of which saturated	3.0g
of which monounsaturated	4.1g
of which polyunsaturated	2.2g
of which total Omega-3	1.9g
of which EPA, DHA	1.5g
Fibre	<0.5g
Sodium	0.21g
equivalent as salt	0.3g

There are four food types that contribute energy and form the bulk of what we eat. These are proteins, fats, carbohydrates and alcohol.

Proteins

We need protein for maintenance and repair of body tissues, such as bones, muscles, cartilage, skin and blood. All proteins are made up of smaller building blocks called amino acids, and the first thing we do when we eat protein is totally break them down into these smaller blocks.

Our body uses a range of different amino acids, and it can make many of them for itself. However, there are nine amino acids that it cannot make, and these must come from our food. Without them, we cannot function properly. These are known as essential amino acids, and foods that contain all of them are called complete proteins.

Examples of foods providing complete proteins include meat, fish, eggs, milk and cheese. Some vegetarian foods such as soy and quinoa also provide complete proteins. Other sources of protein include nuts, beans, lentils, seeds and wheat.

Each gram of pure protein contains 4 kcal of energy.

Fats

Fats are traditionally regarded as evil, especially by some dieters. Many people go on low-fat, low-calorie diets, and this can be a mistake. We need fats not only for energy, but also for insulation of body organs, for transporting some vitamins and other nutrients through the body, for cell integrity and also for making up some of our most important chemicals, such as hormones.

Food labels usually display the total amount of fat in the product, and sometimes also break it down into different types of fat, as in the example above. The breakdown is typically up to four categories, which are called saturated, monounsaturated, polyunsaturated and trans-fats, and it is worth knowing the difference between them.

Saturated fats are usually solid in pure form, such as butter or the fat you find on meat. In reasonably small quantities, they are an essential part of what we need to eat. For example, they help enhance the immune system, but of course they can be harmful if eaten in excess. In particular, this is the main naturally occurring fat that increases insulin resistance.

We have two types of a substance called cholesterol in our bodies. Cholesterol has been given a lot of bad press, and of course excess cholesterol in our blood is extremely unhealthy. But we need a basic amount of it in order for our bodies to function properly, and also to make many of the hormones our body needs. There are various forms of cholesterol, and the two most predominant are the ones which we call 'good cholesterol' or HDL, and 'bad cholesterol' or LDL. The bad cholesterol is associated with heart disease. Excess saturated fats are reported to increase the bad cholesterol in our bodies, and indeed the total level of cholesterol.

Foods that contain saturated fats include milk, yoghurt, cheese, animal fat, whipped cream, pâtés and a large number of processed meats and foods

Unsaturated fats are generally liquid at room temperature. There are two kinds of unsaturated fats.

Monounsaturated fats are one of the 'good guys' when it comes to fats, and these should not be cut out in any diet. These are behind the popular Mediterranean diet, which is claimed to be very healthy. As it has a lot in common with what I swapped in, it is worth a top-level outline of it here. This way of living involves eating mainly unrefined vegetables and fruits, some dairy products such as cheese and yogurt, some fish but little meat. It also includes a high consumption of olive oil. These, especially olive oil, provide a high intake of monounsaturated fats.

Monounsatured fats tend to reduce the level of bad cholesterol.

Foods that contain monounsaturated fats include olives, olive oil, avocados, nuts and seeds.

Polyunsaturated fats are needed in smaller quantities, and they are essential fats in that the body cannot make these for itself.

There are various types of polyunsaturated fats, and the two main ones are called omega-3 and omega-6. While we need both of them, it is important to have a good balance between them, preferably in about equal amounts. Too high a ratio of omega-6 to omega-3 can be linked with various health conditions such as lower immune function, weight gain and even increased risk of cancer. Also, importantly, it is thought to increase insulin resistance. In addition, it can be linked to heart disease, and very importantly to me, reduced operation of the brain. It is a sign of our times, and the food industry, that omega-3 is becoming increasingly scarce. For example, eggs used to contain as much omega-3 as omega-6, and we now find commercial supermarket eggs containing 15 times more omega-6 than omega-3.

Foods that contain a high level of omega-6 and a relatively low level of omega-3 include vegetable oils and anything deep-fried in them. Our modern processed food is very high in omega-6, and some manufacturers even display this as if it were a good thing.

One of the food labels shown earlier is for relatively unprocessed salmon, and shows that the polyunsaturated fat contains a very high percentage of omega-3. The label also shows the amounts of EPA and DHA, which are the variants of omega-3 thought to be the healthiest. This is a food I would definitely buy.

Foods that are high in omega-3 include fresh oily fish, such as sardines, tuna, mackerel and salmon, and flax and chia seeds.

Note that while fresh tuna contains a high level of omega-3, tinned tuna hardly contains any at all. As is all too common, the more highly processed any food is, the more of its nutrients are removed as a result.

Trans-fats are often referred to as partially hydrogenated fats. They are man-made products, formed by forcing hydrogen into polyunsaturated fats such as vegetable oils. This process creates a variety of fat that just does not occur naturally, and our bodies do not know what to do with it. The result is increased insulin resistance, and increased risk of heart disease. Trans-fats increase the bad cholesterol, and decrease the good, which is where the risk of heart attack comes from. Trans-fats are the most harmful of all of the fats, and the most important to reduce to an absolute minimum.

Foods that contain high levels of trans-fats include margarine, shortening, packaged biscuits and cakes, pies, and especially fried fast food.

Fats contain more than double the energy of protein, and each gram of fat contains about 9 kcal. This may be one reason why many diet fads avoid all fats, as there is a higher amount of calories in a smaller amount of fat.

Carbohydrates

We need carbohydrates for energy. No matter what kind of carbohydrate is eaten, it eventually gets converted into a form of sugar called glucose. Glucose fuels body movements including heartbeats and breathing, and also the brain. Indeed, glucose is the only source of energy that the brain uses, and if there is not enough glucose in the blood, it can lead to blackout, coma or even be fatal.

A simple carbohydrate consists of one, or only a few, sugar molecules connected together. When these are eaten, they cause glucose to enter into the bloodstream very quickly. Complex carbohydrates have increasing numbers of sugar molecules strung together, and they release glucose into the bloodstream a lot more slowly. In general, the more complex the carbohydrate, the more slowly the sugar enters the bloodstream.

Foods that contain simple carbohydrates include everything containing sugar, or a widespread ingredient called high fructose corn syrup, such as doughnuts, cakes, biscuits, many fizzy soft drinks, concentrated fruit juices, and most breakfast cereals.

Foods that are a little more complex and still release sugar quite quickly include white bread, white rice, pizza base and especially soft burger buns.

Foods consisting of complex carbohydrates include unprocessed oats, wholegrain bread, wholemeal pasta, grains, vegetables such as beans and other pulses, corn, and broccoli. In general, even for foods with complex carbohydrates, the more processed they are, the simpler they become, and the more quickly they trigger a release of sugar into the blood.

Carbohydrates contain 4 kcal/gram, just like proteins, and this is totally independent of whether the carbohydrate is simple or complex.

Alcohol

Many social and cultural interactions and celebrations involve drinking alcohol. While there is a debate over whether a glass of wine every now and then is actually good for you, alcohol itself has no nutritional value whatsoever, and of course in excess can have only harmful effects.

Each gram of pure alcohol contains 7 kcal. It is common to measure alcohol in units, and each unit represents about eight grams of pure alcohol, and provides 56 kcal. Units are normally printed on the bottle, and can also be derived from the published strength of the drink. As an example, a 5% lager means that 5% of the volume of the drink is pure alcohol. You may see it referred to as 5% ABV (alcohol by volume). The number of units for a drink of a known number of millilitres is:

(Strength in ABV) x (number of mls) / 1000

As an example, a pint (568 ml) of 5% lager is 5 * 568 / 1000, which is 2.8 units. This provides 158 kcal from the alcohol alone, plus almost 100 kcal more from the sugars and other carbohydrates and chemicals in the lager. It is recommended that males should not drink more than three to four units per day, and for females it is two to three units per day. Excess alcohol has been shown to increase insulin resistance, but moderate drinking can easily be part of the lifestyle choices you make.

In addition to the energy-producing nutrients, there are four other important nutrients worth mentioning to help make the most informed choices.

Minerals

Minerals are typically chemical elements which play a role in the structure and operation of the body. One example is calcium which plays a role in muscle movements, and is also part of the building blocks for teeth and bones. Another is iron, which is needed for the blood to do its job properly.

One interesting case is sodium, which is a constituent of common salt. We need this to function. Indeed, the term 'salary' for our wages comes from a popular, but possibly distorted, story that the Romans used to give out salt to their soldiers for their survival. But too much salt can raise the blood pressure. There is so much salt in processed food that it is nearly impossible to have too low an intake. The challenge is to keep it within healthy levels.

There are many minerals we need in very small quantities, and each one plays its role in the body. In general, minerals come from fresh food and a wide range of vegetables.

Vitamins

Vitamins are special organic compounds that your body needs in very small quantities to allow you to function normally. You must get these from food as your body can't make them from scratch.

Vitamins A, C and E are antioxidants, which are substances that help protect your cells against the effects of free radicals which are always present in the body. These vitamins have many other roles in maintaining the immune system and other bodily functions, and are present in most fruits and vegetables.

Vitamin B is a family of eight different vitamins which are vital for a whole range of things, including skin, nerves, blood and general metabolism. They can be found in a wide range of meat, fish and vegetables. Note the items in the 'Vitamins and iron' section of the cereal biscuit food label above. All of them, except of course iron, are actually members of the vitamin B family, which have been added to make the product appear more nutritious.

Vitamin D helps keep bones strong, and is thought to help fight cancer. We get this from dairy foods, cereals that are fortified with vitamin D, and fatty fish like salmon. We also make it for ourselves if we are exposed to sunlight.

Vitamin K helps make some of the necessary proteins in the body, and is also involved in building bone. As it is in so many foods, most people will get enough of this unless they eat only junk food all the time.

Vitamins B and C are soluble in water, and are quickly excreted from the body. As a result, these vitamins do not get stored (with the exception of B_{12}), and it is therefore best to ensure food choices such as fruit and vegetables that provide these vitamins every day. Vitamins A, D, E and K can be stored in fat and your liver.

Phytochemicals

Phytochemicals are natural plant chemicals that help the body and the immune system protect itself against high blood pressure and diseases such as cancer, diabetes and heart disease. The high antioxidant quality of many of these is even thought to slow down the effects of aging. Almost 1,000 different phytochemicals have been identified in food, and many of them are responsible for giving the plant its colour.

The word itself means 'chemicals derived from plants' and these are found in all fruit and vegetables, especially highly coloured varieties.

Fibre

Fibre consists of extremely complex carbohydrates, or cellulose, which are not converted to sugar at all, and there are two forms. Insoluble fibre does not dissolve in water, and does not provide any energy whatsoever in the form of calories. Soluble fibre dissolves in water, and is digested very slowly. It does in the end provide a little energy, but not in the form of sugar, and far lower kcal/gram than true carbohydrates.

Fibre is important not only because it is healthy for the digestive system and also for reducing cholesterol in the blood, but it slows down the release of sugar into the blood from other foods. Perhaps equally importantly, it provides a feeling of satisfaction when eaten, which can last for a lot longer than foods without fibre. It actually reduces the appetite in a natural and healthy way.

Fibre only occurs in plant-based foods such as fruit and vegetables. In general, the more processed the food (e.g. white bread, white rice), the lower the amount of fibre it contains. This is over and above the additional effect of processing that reduces the complexity of the carbohydrates, and produces foods which put sugar into the blood more quickly.

Foods containing fibre include oats and other cereals, bran, nuts, seeds, potato skin and beans.

Water

Water is essential for your health, and for your full metabolism. A healthy amount to drink is around six to eight glasses a day, which is a total of two to three pints. If you do not give your body enough water, it fights back and tries to store it. It also does not allow you to burn up the fat in your cells as effectively either.

It is also claimed that some of modern society's health problems would be far less severe if we all drank the right amount of water, and that we do our bodies, our health and our metabolism a lot of harm by depriving ourselves of enough pure water. If you wait until you notice you are thirsty, you are already slightly dehydrated. So it might be a good idea to build the habit of drinking water even if you are not thirsty. I built in a habit of drinking two glasses of water before breakfast to start my day in a state of good hydration, and aim to drink more during the day.

Thirst is often signalled to the brain with messages that are often mistaken for hunger. So, drinking water in response to feelings of hunger might be more than just filling the stomach, or more than tricking yourself into getting rid of the hunger; it might actually be the response that your body is looking for.

A note on diets

A typical approach to handling either or both excess weight and Type 2 diabetes is to go on a diet. We are bombarded with programmes and magazines that extol the virtues of particular diets. Some people go from one diet to another, often feeling like failures and wondering why they don't succeed.

There is of course a place for diets, but the dieting process has a few traps that it is easy to fall into.

The first is that one 'goes on a diet', and thinking this way, the only next step is to 'come off the diet', whether successful or not. There is often little thought about what you do once you have had a successful diet, unless it is a diet for life. There are of course healthy diets for life, and they deserve to be successful. However, the mainstream dieting industry seems to favour specific restrictions.

Some diets are of the type where you focus on only one food, such as cabbage soup or baby food, or any other single item of food. This cannot possibly sustain anyone for the rest of their life. Other diets focus on totally cutting out a major food type, such as fats or carbohydrates. Still others focus on reducing calorie intake to a near minimum. In general, these are unhealthy and unsustainable, with the possible exception of low-carbohydrate diets which will be discussed later. Many of them may appear successful for a short time, and that is of course where much of the appeal is. We hear of people on certain diets that lose ten pounds in one or two weeks, and it can look seductively attractive. But it can take enormous willpower, and in the longer term is unlikely to have a payback and can even be counterproductive.

Some people go on extremely low-calorie diets. Such a crash diet appears to work well at first. When starved, the body starts using the glucose stored in the liver, and you soon run these stores empty. This glucose is stored with water, so as the glucose is used up, the water is released. You could easily lose seven pounds in the first week, or even more.

But your body is geared for survival. It sends signals to the brain that set the feeling of hunger to a new height. It slows down your metabolism so you burn fat more slowly, and starts using up muscle to get its energy. When you finally break your diet and resume normal eating, you will gain more weight and store the fat even more effectively than before.

It is instructive to consider a typical fad diet, where the dieter loses weight and then regains it again, possibly in a cycle repeated like a yo-yo many times over. A typically restrictive diet can cause the muscle tissue to be used up as part of the weight loss. So imagine someone at 100 kg who very quickly gets to 80 kg, and loses 1 kg of muscle tissue as a direct result. Never mind, they are now at 80 kg and feeling good about themselves. Then either they give up or simply find it difficult to maintain and somehow slide back to their original weight. I know from experience how easy this is to do. If they have lost 1 kg of muscle tissue, they will not regain it when the diet stops unless they specifically work towards doing it. This means that when they get back to 100 kg, they are actually carrying an extra kilogram of fat. Remembering that what sensible dieters really want to lose is not weight, but fat, they are actually worse off than they were before. This will make it just a little bit more difficult to reduce the weight next time round. If this becomes a roller-coaster cycle, you drain yourself both physically and emotionally, and achieve the very opposite of what you were intending. This is definitely not a formula for health and fitness. In summary, yo-yo dieting can be the result of overly restrictive and unsupervised dieting practices, and can actually be counterproductive.

This does not mean there is no place for diets. There are many cases where someone with severe Type 2 diabetes has under medical supervision, or even following surgery to force a permanent reduction in food intake, either mitigated or totally reversed their diabetes. Also a short-term, 'short sharp shock' diet can work well and be appropriate under some circumstances, especially if it is an integral short-term part of a long-term plan or commitment.

Having said that, a lifestyle change towards a healthy balance of the different energy nutrients described above is probably more likely to succeed than adopting any kind of restrictive diet. Especially if you can give a confident and resounding "Yes" to the question "Can I live the rest of my life doing this?"

Eating – a balanced perspective

It is easy to simply say that one should have a balanced way of eating, but what does that mean and how does one do it? The subject of nutrition is very complex, and the earlier section deliberately only scratches the surface of what is really there. There is a lot of conflicting advice, often in the form of different food pyramids and plate contents saying what ratios and proportions you should and should not be eating. These do not seem to take into account the level of exercise that a person is doing, nor their weight or muscle mass. In addition, modern research is challenging some of the conventional advice given by health departments, particularly the high percentage of carbohydrates that are currently recommended.

Also, people have different metabolisms; some do well with a high carbohydrate ratio and others on a high protein ratio. It does not look like there is a 'one size fits all' answer.

My approach was reasonably simple. That was to build an idea of what foods are helpful in achieving and maintaining the target, and which foods are unhelpful, and maybe slowly, but definitely surely, swap them out. And to trust that eating a reasonable quantity of healthier food is better than eating a similar quantity of highly processed or junk food.

And using the mental tools to make sure that what you eat and how much you eat is always a choice you take willingly and mindfully, so that eating the right quantities for you eventually becomes automatic and not a punishing imposition.

So, let's set up a few guidelines based on understanding the nutrients, and also from an insulin perspective. Hopefully it is becoming increasingly clear that habits which cause there to be too much insulin in the body are counterproductive, and choices that will keep the insulin level as low as possible will help guide you to success. This is at least as important as calorie consumption.

The very worst possible combination is that of high levels of simple carbohydrates that enter the body quickly, doubly so when accompanied by saturated fat. Typical examples are doughnuts, cakes, biscuits and many fast food takeaways such as pizza or food in soft burger buns and French fries, especially with sweet fizzy soft drinks. Indeed, most of the ever-available fast foods are like this. When these are eaten, especially in large quantities, the resulting high level of insulin will trigger the storage of all of these as fat in your body.

The amount of sugar that gets put into the bloodstream can be regarded as something called the glycaemic load of the food. There are lists of numbers measuring how quickly pure foods release sugar into the bloodstream, called the glycaemic index. It is tempting to put such a list in the book, but while important, this is not the only crucial number. Let us illustrate this by considering eating a spoonful of honey. If eaten alone, it will quickly enter the bloodstream. However, if mixed in with say pure oat porridge, the fibre, bulk and complex carbohydrates will slow down the sugar release. Fats and proteins have a similar slowing effect. So what is important is the glycaemic load of the whole meal, and it is worth knowing which foods have a low or a high glycaemic load. A breakdown of a variety of foods, including percentages of protein, carbohydrate, fats and an indicator of glycaemic load, are presented in Appendices 1 and 2. Many of these numbers can be seen for yourself while in the supermarket.

Having said all this, whether you choose to learn about the details of nutrition or not, you can make general guidelines to help choose for yourself what to swap out and what to replace it with.

If you understand the general rules, you will be able to make better choices. As a broad brush view, 'good food' is typically fresh fruit, fresh vegetables and beans, grain, seeds, fish and non-fatty meat, and 'bad food' is typically cakes, sweets, modern fast food, and highly processed food containing a lot of fat and sugars. Also, low-glycaemic meals and snacks are much better than high-glycaemic meals.

So some suggested swap-outs might be:

▶ Fast food for meat or fish with vegetables

▶ Highly processed foods for less processed foods. For example, white bread swapped out for wholemeal or preferably wholegrain bread, or cakes and biscuits for fruit

- Sweetened cereals for low-sugar muesli or oats
- Cakes and croissants for eggs or wholemeal toast
- Fizzy sweet drinks for chilled sparkling water
- French fries, crisps and potatoes for a variety of vegetables of different colours. Some people say 'eat a rainbow' of fruit and vegetables to make sure you get a healthy choice and all the nutrients your body needs

You can go a long way with just this kind of swap-out, knowing that each decision will provide more nutrients, lower sugar spikes, and in the end greater satiety for the same number of calories. This can be done while retaining your level of choice all the way along the journey.

Note that a lot of traps have been set for you. Here is a small set of examples to be wary of:

- Many healthy-looking sandwiches and wraps available for lunches, such as tuna, chicken or egg, often contain a high level of mayonnaise and other oils. Such sandwiches typically contain 15-25% fat. It is instructive to look at the food labels to see the total calories and particularly the amount of fat.
- Oats are a good complex carbohydrate which releases sugar slowly into the body. But beware of packaged instant oats where you just add hot water. These are usually refined to make them much simpler and also have a lot of extra sugar added.
- Manufacturers do not have to put the amount of trans-fats on labels if less than 0.5% and can claim it is zero.
- 'Healthy' food options often hide the real truth. Reduced sugar often means increased fat and/or reduced fibre, and vice versa. One brand of potato crisps offers a reduced fat version, which contains a third less fat, but at the expense of significantly increasing the glycaemic load. This means that the so-called healthier option will in fact pump 50% more sugar into your blood.

▶ Beware of those foods that say they are 85% fat-free. This means they contain 15% fat, which by itself contributes a massive 135 kcals for every 100g of the product, and probably well over 50% of the calories in the product come from the fat.

▶ Portion sizes on food labels are often quoted per 100g. But some food labels quote only amount per serving, sometimes not clearly indicating what size a serving is. It can often be as low as 10 or 20 grams, making it look like it contains fewer calories than it actually does.

▶ Many innocent-looking dips are packed with calories and fat, often using mayonnaise. For example, taramasalata can contain over 500 kcals per 100g, and mayonnaise itself 680. Here is where a salsa dip comes into its own, and can be as low as 60 kcals per 100g. The calorie values of some different dips are shown in Appendix 3.

▶ Some fast food outlets serve salads which they claim to be healthy alternatives. The Caesar salad from one popular outlet is over 700 kcals, which if served with a large fizzy drink takes it up to 1,000 kcals. In particular, be wary of the mayonnaise, cheese sauces and croutons that come with such salads.

It is a good habit to become vigilant of food labels to help avoid some of these traps. However, some labels are designed to deceive you, and some have been shown to be quite incorrect. One way to avoid many of the traps is to move towards less processed and more unrefined foods, as is part of the theme of this chapter.

An important part of a balanced perspective is in the ratio of the main nutrients. Health guidelines suggest that a normal healthy balanced eating is around 55% carbohydrates, 30% fat and 15% protein. It is interesting to note that ever since obesity rates started to go up, we have been eating an increasingly lower percentage of fat, and instead we are eating an increasingly higher percentage of carbohydrates. The mounting evidence suggests that the obesity and diabetes explosion is fuelled by modern-day carbohydrates, and that a lower percentage of carbohydrate could be very beneficial, *especially* to people with insulin resistance.

There are some diets that prescribe a very low percentage of carbohydrates indeed, which means eating mainly high protein and high fat, and they do seem to work well for some people. In the spirit of not restricting myself, I have not chosen to adopt this strict kind of diet, but have been happy to make it a habit to eat lower carbohydrate, higher protein and also somewhat higher fat choices such as eggs with breakfast, avocado with my salad, and fish or meat most evenings with rarely any sweet puddings afterwards, and small amounts of nuts and seeds with snacks.

Following these simple swapping-out ideas will bring your food intake much closer to a healthy balance, help you become more satisfied with healthy amounts, and also increase all the other nutrients described above.

Sweet tooth, and large appetite

I was in a hospital ward when breakfast was being served. One of the patients had Type 2 diabetes, and had just taken his morning dose of Metformin, a drug designed to keep the blood sugar level down. He was offered tea and said, "Yes please, with two sugars." He looked at the tea lady, smiled and said, "I have a sweet tooth." I did not say anything, but was somewhat saddened at the thought of how his diabetes was likely to progress while he had that mindset.

Some people label themselves as having a sweet tooth. Remember that you were not born with this, but it got programmed into you along the way, perhaps when you were very young. If you have been enjoying sweet food for a long time, it can initially appear a great challenge to stop. However, some compromise has to be reached if you are seriously looking at a lifestyle change.

If you have been taking sugar in tea or coffee, perhaps here is an opportunity to start phasing it out. In the spirit of 'Don't stop – swap' you *could* use artificial sweeteners. This may appear to be a good first step. The research in this area gives mixed results and conclusions, but apart from any long-term concerns about taking these chemicals, it appears that the sweet taste can fool the body into producing insulin to deal with the sugar it thinks it is taking in. This puts the blood sugar level out of balance by lowering it, and this can increase the feeling of hunger later. Some research shows that people taking sweeteners instead of sugar can lose weight more effectively; some shows that people who take in a large amount of calorie-free diet drinks can actually gain weight as a result.

Perhaps the healthiest thing is to start reducing your taste for sweet things in general. This is so pivotal a change that it might be the one thing worth considering dealing with head-on.

If you take two spoons of sugar, start by cutting it out or perhaps going to one, and begin to get used to the new experience of the taste. Your coffee will have a different taste, and you might find you actually learn to appreciate it more. Or for those that drink tea, there are many types of tea such as green jasmine tea whose taste can be best appreciated without cluttering it up with sugar. If you aim to eliminate sugar completely, either immediately or over say a month or two, you will have significantly reduced your calorie intake and sugar spikes, and have started the process of taming the sweet tooth – or swapping it for something different.

It would also show that such habits can be broken, even if perhaps with a little difficulty at first. This is one that is really worth going for, as it could underpin many healthy future choices, and indeed make the whole programme easier to succeed and maintain.

If you already don't take sugar in your beverages, choose something similar which can be beneficial to eliminate – perhaps replacing fizzy soft drinks with fizzy water, or cake with fruit. Reducing the desire for artificially or overly sweet foods will help you swap out more easily and naturally later on.

So far, the focus has been on *what* food to change. Now just a note on the *amount*.

It is common for people to eat until they are totally full up at the end of the meal. I used to do that, and only say I was satisfied when I got to this point. A good habit to get into is to eat enough so that there is just a *tiny* space left, or until you know that you will be satisfied in 20 minutes' time as you start to digest your food. This is being satisfied as distinct from being full up. You could think of this as just being a tiny way out of your comfort zone.

As you do this over a period of time, your comfort zone will expand, and your appetite will shrink a little, especially if you are also eating more healthy foods.

You are not fighting against your appetite here – rigid control does not usually work well in the long term. You are simply and slowly reducing your appetite, so that in the long run you eat what you want, and want what you eat. Eventually, you may find that you will feel uncomfortable, even bloated, if you eat too much at any time. And when this happens, you could smile and think 'Good! This is how I *want* to feel when I overeat.'

Activity and exercise

So far the focus has been on changing eating habits, with respect to what kind of food is eaten, and how much. Reducing weight by healthy eating certainly has a positive effect on lowering insulin resistance.

Now the focus will be on physical activity and exercise. This is a crucial part of the lifestyle change, and it also has a lot of other benefits.

The first, and most widely understood, is that activity burns up calories. So the combination of changing eating habits in conjunction with exercise habits actually makes any weight reduction programme a lot easier to do, and also to maintain.

The second one is that almost every muscle movement takes sugar out of the bloodstream, so the greater the amount of activity, the more you potentially lower your blood sugar.

Perhaps the major benefit from a diabetic perspective is that as underused muscles become insensitive to insulin, exercise plays a major role in reducing insulin resistance. A good exercise programme could eventually restore most or all of the insulin response. So exercise is a crucial part of reversing Type 2 diabetes.

There are lots of other benefits too in moving from a sedentary lifestyle and building in activity.

Exercise builds the strength of the heart, and your resting heart rate will become lower as each single beat pumps more blood around the body. Average resting heart rates might be 70 beats/minute, and a good exercise routine can reduce this to 60 beats/minute, or even lower.

Exercise also tends to lower blood pressure, reduce the bad cholesterol in your blood and increase the level of good cholesterol, which helps reduce the risk of heart disease. Of course lowering your blood sugar and insulin will add to this.

Many types of exercise strengthen the bones. As we start to lose bone density, and as a result bone strength, from the age of 30, these will also help reduce the possibility of brittle bones for the future. Also our joints need movement to keep them functioning properly and at their full range of movement.

Another benefit of exercise is that it can trigger the release of chemicals in the body called endorphins which promote a sense of well-being and can also reduce the feeling of hunger. This can help you feel better and sleep more soundly, and either reduce your stress or increase your ability to handle some of life's challenges in a more resourceful way. This is surely an important part of having a good life.

Getting started

This section is designed for people who have been inactive, and may also be overweight, and perhaps be 40 years or older. However, age is no barrier and even people in their seventies or eighties can achieve much better fitness and reduce their insulin resistance.

Starting an exercise programme suddenly can be risky, and it is important to start it safely. We made a distinction between increasing normal everyday activity, and starting a specific exercise programme.

One place to start safely is by increasing your normal everyday activity. For instance, walk a little more often and maybe a little more briskly. Or take the stairs, or walk up escalators. Or move even while watching television, perhaps getting up during adverts to switch channels or maybe get a glass of water. These are all everyday movements which your body already does on a routine basis, and they would be done at an intensity that is unlikely to cause any undue stress to the body or heart. Whatever you decide to do as a habit to start and maintain extra movement and activity will help provide a good foundation.

Let us imagine someone tries to reduce their weight by six pounds per month using exercise alone, whilst not changing their food intake in any way. As it takes 3,500 kcals for each pound of fat loss, this requires increasing their physical activity by a further 750 kcal/day every day. Suppose this is done purely by walking. An 80 kg person would need to walk about 7.5 miles every day to achieve this, or have to do very intensive exercise for 60-90 minutes each and every day. Although possible, this is likely to be an unachievable and unmaintainable programme for most people. I have seen active people try to achieve this, and following a burst of enthusiasm, not succeeded in the medium term.

Now suppose you decided to aim for around 300 kcal/day of extra activity. If it were only done via walking, this would probably be a three-mile walk which can of course be split up into shorter sessions, perhaps three walks to and from somewhere only half a mile away. Unless the pace is quite brisk, this is likely to take just under an hour. This would be an excellent start for a weight-reduction programme, especially if combined with a slight decrease of calorie intake. If all is well, this might possibly be sufficient to reduce your insulin resistance if maintained throughout and after the target weight reduction. However, there is more that can be done, especially as this level of intensity is not usually enough to fully programme the muscles to develop insulin sensitivity, which is another way of describing reducing insulin resistance.

If you want to develop better insulin sensitivity by extending the exercise programme up to or beyond this point, it is wise to make sure you start safely.

If you are on any diabetic medication such as insulin, or anything that triggers insulin secretion, such as sulphonylureas, it is important to consult your doctor and make sure you agree what is necessary to ensure your blood sugar does not go too low. Whether this is done by careful monitoring, or a slight reduction of medication, or even ratcheting it down under the doctor's agreement and supervision, will be an individual decision. Either way, it is important to have some emergency carbohydrates with you such as glucose gels or a sugared drink until you are confident that you have reached a new balance between exercise, sugar level and medication.

Even if you are not on medication, it is important to inform your doctor that you intend to embark on a programme of increased exercise, and to have a full medical check-up to determine whether there are any indications of risk. In my case this was not necessary as my doctor had as good as ordered me to start one.

At this point, there are a lot of choices. However you start, it is very important to choose something you like doing, or can imagine eventually enjoying. If you heroically struggle on a treadmill for 20 minutes or running in the street hating every minute of it, you are unlikely to maintain it, unless for example you feel inspired by the idea of eventually becoming a good runner. One of my friends did just that as part of a recovery from cancer and now loves running marathons, but his courage and determination are quite uncommon. I certainly couldn't have done this.

One choice is to start regularly doing specific sports or activities, such as brisk or Nordic walking, running, cycling, swimming, tennis, golf, gardening, or dancing. There is a tremendous range of choices here. The number of kcal/hour you would use up for these and some other activities is shown in Appendix 5. Doing such exercise, particularly with an exercise partner or as part of an exercise or activity group, can be motivating and help keep the programme on track.

Another is to join a gym, and make sure that you are set a programme that fits your needs. This would include making sure you learn to warm up, cool down, and do some specific stretching exercises to maintain suppleness and also minimise the possibility of damaging your muscles. A warm up means starting by doing lighter exercise than the session would demand, so the muscles and joints are ready to take on the session. A cool down is to gradually slow down at the end of the session so that the heart rate comes down slowly, and the muscles start closing down slowly enough to minimise any later aching or damage. The classes in a gym should always contain these components, and all good gyms should provide an induction programme so that you learn how to do the exercises with good technique, which is important to make sure there are no unintentional injuries.

Yet another is to engage a personal trainer, who will design and monitor a programme that will help you achieve your goals. This could be, but does not have to be, in a gym. It could be in your house, your garden, a park, or any other place where you can exercise in private if you choose to. If you are very overweight or starting from scratch, and especially if you are diabetic, it is worth choosing a trainer with a qualification in GP Referral and preferably also in Obesity and Diabetes. Any good personal trainer will ask you to see your doctor first and get signed medical approval, and might not be prepared to take you on until this has been done. This is not an insult, but shows that the personal trainer is acting responsibly and professionally, and in your best interests and safety.

A healthy adult who is aiming to remain healthy or do activity as part of a weight reduction programme is advised by national guidelines to aim for at least 30 minutes of moderate intensity physical activity on at least five days a week. This is in line with the

300 kcal/day programme outlined above, including the idea that this can be spread out into shorter activity periods throughout the day. A moderate level of activity would make you a little warmer, and make you breathe more heavily, but not so much that you cannot talk due to the effort of breathing. A brisk or uphill walk would do this very nicely. If starting a programme with the intention of reducing blood sugar level, 45 minutes a day would be an even better target to aim for.

If apart from fitness level you are otherwise healthy, you can see there is a wide range of choice. If you have some constraints such as an injury or disability, then it may look more daunting at first sight. One of my friends had damaged his knees many years ago doing sports. When faced with the need to reduce his weight and blood sugar significantly, he chose low-impact but high-intensity exercises such as the elliptical cross-trainer, rowing machine and stationary bike. Another of my friends had her leg amputated below the knee as a result of cancer treatment. She now swims regularly with an artificial limb, and recently swam a mile non-stop for charity. The Paralympics also show what can be achieved in the face of adversity.

Whatever you decide, it is best to make an initial decision and get started. You can always review and adapt your decision at any point.

Up and running

When starting an exercise programme from scratch, it can sometimes take some effort to find the momentum to start exercising successfully on a regular basis, especially if your lifestyle has been mainly sedentary until now. However, once you are in motion, it is much easier to do other activities than if you have been static. There is an almost paradoxical saying: 'If you want something done, give it to a busy person.' Exercise can be like that too. When slouched on the sofa, not having moved for an hour, it can sometimes seem too much effort to drag yourself up and start doing something active. However, once you are up on your feet, moving around, it is one step easier to pick up and get started. The mental exercise in this section may help prepare for this.

While in a relaxed state as described earlier in the book, imagine being asked to do something while you are lying down and doing nothing, or have been sitting for a couple of hours perhaps idly watching television. The task could even be something as simple and effortless as getting up and switching a light on or off. It could be quite an effort to begin doing it even if it is really an easy thing you are being asked.

Now imagine you are being asked to do the same thing, but you are already up and actively in the middle of doing some activity. It usually feels like much less effort to move to that light switch, or in general fit something in once you are in an 'up and running' state. Check out for yourself the difference between the two feelings.

Now remember a time when you were sitting down and then chose to stand up and start doing things, and feeling even better and more fulfilled afterwards as a result. Perhaps you appreciated the sedentary state even more after returning from the activity and sitting or lying down again. In that context, you could think of it as a resting state. If there is any difficulty in remembering such a time, just go ahead and imagine one. Then imagine doing this at various times in the future.

So, if the sedentary period is not genuine rest or relaxation, or not an intentional stillness such as meditation, it is often better to stand up and start moving about to help create enough momentum to actually start doing a planned exercise session. And even if you don't specifically exercise at that time, the 'up and running' state can be so much healthier and satisfying in the longer term. This could be a good general decision to make if you are starting an exercise programme from scratch.

Progression with cardiovascular exercise

Once you have made a start, it is worth considering whether or how you wish to progress. There may be various reasons why you might want to do this.

It could be to help accelerate any weight reduction programme, or to decrease your blood sugar level further. It might be that the activity itself starts to be enjoyable, or there is a wish to get better in some way especially if there is a competitive aspect to the chosen activity.

Perhaps one of the reasons might be to pull down any remaining insulin resistance that might still be there, especially if the blood sugar level has not fallen to the point you had wanted. This means further reducing the insulin resistance, much of which comes from your muscles.

The programme outlined in the above section is a minimum guideline for a healthy heart and body. The fat reduction and increased use of muscles will start to decrease insulin resistance. In many cases, especially for people with prediabetic blood sugar levels, the weight reduction and increased activity will be enough to have a noticeable effect on your blood sugar, and might even bring it down below prediabetic levels. The higher the initial blood sugar levels, the more that needs to be done to bring them back to normal. So if you want to turn the ratchet further on insulin resistance, or simply start to enjoy the sensation of being fit and wish to develop that, it is useful to understand some other forms of exercise that can help make this happen.

Firstly, the body is extremely adaptable. If you exercise a muscle, it will get stronger. If you don't exercise a muscle, it will gradually become weaker and smaller, and less ready to respond to insulin. This is why regular exercise is important, so that the benefits are maintained, and also all-round exercise that works as many different muscles as possible.

There are two main categories of exercise that work the muscles, burn calories and decrease insulin resistance, and they are called cardiovascular exercises (often called cardio) and resistance exercises. A good exercise routine, especially for insulin, is a combination of both.

Cardiovascular exercise consists of usually rhythmic continuous exercise that if performed at high intensity significantly increases your heart rate and your breathing. Examples are running, cycling, rowing, swimming, dancing, football, tennis, and using the elliptical cross-trainer or stepper machines in the gym. If you wish to progress with these, there are a few considerations to follow.

The first is your heart rate. There is a very crude formula that indicates what your absolute maximum heart rate should be, and that is:

Maximum heart rate in beats/minute = 220 – Age in years

So if you are 30, your maximum heart rate would be 190 beats/minute, and if you are 60 it would be 160 beats/minute. This number represents the heart rate you would get with the maximum possible exertion, and is unlikely to be attained in everyday life. It is also fair to say that this is a very great generalisation as many people deviate from this by 20 beats/minute or even more, and this can also vary with your level of cardiac fitness. So it is nothing more than a rule of thumb.

In general, light cardiovascular exercise will keep your heart rate below 65% of maximum, moderate exercise between 65% and 75%, and vigorous or intense exercise above 75-80%. It is useful to aim to build up to 70-75% to start with. If you are not used to exercise, it won't take very much to raise your heart rate to this level, and as you get more and more fit, you can do an ever-increasing amount before reaching this rate.

You can determine your heart rate with a standard heart rate monitor, which you wear like a watch. Or more simply, put your fingers on your neck or wrist and count how many beats there are in 20 seconds and multiply by three. It might not be good to count for a minute as the heart rate starts to slow down and this might give a less accurate and lower result.

A second consideration is how intense you perceive the exercise is. There are various methods, one of the simplest being to assign a number to gauge your level of effort using a scale of 1 to 10: 1 would be very light indeed, 3 is moderate, 5 is strong, 7 is very strong, and 10 is an absolute maximum which can only be maintained for seconds.

As you progress, then for a given level of exercise such as walking one kilometre in 12 minutes, your heart rate might reach 75% of maximum heart rate if you are not used to this level of exercise. Over a period of time it will become increasingly lower on completion, perhaps reducing to 68%. What you once regarded as an intensity level of 6 might now feel like a 4. When this happens, the next step for progressing would be to go slightly faster, or further, or uphill, so that your heart rate and perceived exertion match the original values, and so the cycle of progression continues.

Doing activity at a level of 60% will of course consume calories if enough is done, but doing the same amount of activity at 75%, even if for a shorter time, will help prime the body to lower insulin resistance.

Even better still for insulin reduction is interval training, where you would have an intense burst for 10-20 seconds at maybe level 8-9, and then take it down to 3-6 for 20-60 seconds, a few times in a row. This is more advanced, and if you are new to this it is important to get help and advice from someone who can guide you to do it safely and effectively.

As you start to reach these higher levels of effort, another of your rewards is the release of chemicals in the body called endorphins that promote a feeling of well-being. This also reduces the level of insulin in the body.

You may find that your resting heart rate decreases when taking up a cardiovascular programme. For example, it could be 70 beats/minute before starting an exercise programme, and fall closer to 60 or even below. This is in fact very healthy, and a sign of your increasing fitness.

Progression with resistance exercise

Some people manage very well on pure cardiovascular exercise, and it is certainly good for the heart, the circulation, and for consuming calories.

It is also useful to do resistance exercises, for lots of different reasons. They tend to strengthen the muscles, strengthen the bones, increase your metabolism so that your body uses more calories a day, and also reduce insulin resistance. There are many kinds, including lifting or pushing or pulling weights, or pushing against the weight of your own body, such as press-ups, jumps, pulling yourself up or even stair climbing, which was also mentioned as a cardiovascular exercise. Other resistance exercises can include moving through water, or even just holding weights still against gravity.

Some people avoid resistance exercises because they fear they will bulk up like a body builder. You would have to go out of your way and do a tough set of routines with very heavy weights to get muscles like that, and there is no risk whatsoever of getting large bulges with a modest resistance programme. Indeed, your muscles will simply tone up, and you will look healthier.

As a muscle is challenged, it develops strength and the ability to function better. It also becomes increasingly able to accept insulin. As there are a lot of muscles, it is important to challenge them all, especially the largest muscles in the body. This includes the front and back of the legs, the muscles of the buttocks, chest, back, shoulders, and the front and back of the arms.

The best way to challenge them is in line with the concept of comfort zones, and also similar to progressing with cardiovascular exercise.

As an example, consider lifting and lowering a weighted bar, holding it palms up and bending and straightening your arms, keeping your elbows by your sides. What would be an ideal choice of weight? Some classes ask you to use weights which you can raise and lower to music, maybe 50-100 times in a row. This is good exercise, and will improve your endurance, and is worth doing. However, to really challenge the muscle and bring the insulin resistance down as far as possible, a good weight is one you can lift or lower 8-12 times, and preferably no more than 15. Imagine this weight is 10 kg, and you do two sets of 10 repetitions of lifting and lowering, feeling a slight burn in the muscles, or even finding the last repetition or two quite difficult. As the muscle develops over a few weeks, you could do the same with 11 kg, then 12 kg and so on. Such a routine is called progressive overload, and really gets the muscles going. They will get stronger and firmer, and demand more sugar by becoming increasingly willing to work with your insulin.

A similar strategy would be followed for all the other major muscles. As it is critical to do all of these exercises correctly, I only mention them in passing as it is not easy to do it even from a book that is dedicated to these exercises, and I have seen some very unsafe movements done by people in the gym trying to follow a weights programme from a book or magazine. I would hope you work with someone who can show you properly and feed back on your technique if you choose to go in this direction.

Finally, one can progress a long way without using any weights at all, or having to use machines in a gym, but using low-cost easily portable resistance tubing.

However you choose to exercise your muscles, resistance exercises where the muscles are increasingly challenged just outside the comfort zone is an important ingredient in reducing insulin resistance as low as it can go.

Conclusion

Following an overview of eating and exercise choices, the best way forward is to combine the two. So a twofold method is recommended. Firstly a modest reduction of say 300 kcal of food per day, especially if healthier food is eaten that does not pump sugar into the blood quickly, which will have the side-effect of keeping you feeling less hungry over a longer period of time. Secondly, and in parallel, making an average exertion of 300 kcal of activity per day, also building in some resistance exercises. The combination should reduce excess fat by about a pound a week at first. The more you choose to ratchet up from there, building new habits but still allowing yourself the freedom to taste whatever delights you still like, the more quickly you will start to see the results.

As the programme progresses, you can choose to ratchet down your calorie intake a little at a time, or ratchet up the activity as you become fitter, or even both. As you continue to do this, you will slowly but surely be approaching the maintenance phase.

CHAPTER SIX

The maintenance phase - continuing for life

This chapter looks at the transition between achieving the target and starting to maintain it. It also outlines some of the challenges facing anyone who is making a lifetime journey.

My journey

It is hard to pinpoint exactly when the transition from the achievement phase moved into the maintenance phase. My blood sugar became normal after four to five months, and considering that the whole journey was triggered by the diagnosis of diabetes in the first place, it could be argued that this alone was an achievement. However, my weight continued to reduce, and the fall became slower and slower as it got closer to the target. It was after about 15 months when it appeared to level out at 83 kg. I was initially delighted, and maintained it for about a year.

My new eating habits had become established, and I did not feel at all deprived or imprisoned as I felt that nothing was forbidden, and I could and sometimes did eat less healthy choices. My regular visits to the gym had also become established. For various reasons,

I moved to a larger gym, this time with my daughter who became an exercise companion for three years, until it was time for her to start a new life as a student. There was a nice social atmosphere in the exercise classes, and it was good to see small but continuous improvements in what I was able to achieve physically. This was almost exactly how I envisaged a nice gentle maintenance programme should be.

However, some things happened which changed the balance I had set up, and took me into new territory where I had not ever considered going.

Up to now, I hold up my story as an example which you might choose to follow. The next three paragraphs are definitely not recommendations I would make for the purpose of becoming an ex-diabetic, unless you start to acquire some kind of athletic or competitive aspirations. But I would like to describe it anyway to show how things can change.

My daughter declared we should both do kickboxing classes. I told her, "I am too old to do anything crazy like that," but she insisted, and in the end I went. The first session was at a level of intensity of exercise I had never experienced before, and although I left the class saying "Never again," we did go back. After a while I became a regular member and started grading and getting a collection of coloured belts. During that time, the gym used to run challenges that were open to the members. A particular one was a round of 10 tough exercises, including a chest press lifting and lowering a 40 kg weighted bar 40 times. One of the staff, Adam, asked me if I was going to do the challenge, and I told him "No way," explaining that it was impossible for me to even lift this kind of weight once, never mind what was required for the challenge. Adam started to show me that it was indeed possible, as long as I used good technique, only did a few raises at a time, and rested before the next batch. A similar approach was also taken with the other exercises. Under Adam's instruction, I gradually built up the ability to do them all. One weightlifter in the competition laughed at my efforts, and threw a weight into the air that I could hardly lift. But I was not trying to win, and simply wanted to pace myself on the five cardio and five resistance exercises so that I could complete the circuit. However, on the day, and to my absolute amazement, I did the ten exercises faster than all the other competitors in the gym, and won the challenge.

Suddenly, exercise was no longer just for maintenance. I *enjoyed* being physically fit, and started doing it for its own sake. It really had moved from something I did because it was part of damage control, to something where I was developing and flourishing. My level of fitness soared, and I started feeling younger with each passing year. The sheer impossibility of me doing kickboxing grading and also winning the gym challenge propelled me into a phase of almost five years of choosing things that seemed impossible, and conquering them. My weight decreased, and I loved it, and wanted more. I became hooked on achievement, and even faced one of my past ghosts, generated by being punished at school by having to run. The next project was a half-marathon run, and it is hard to describe the feeling of elation following the final sprint though the finishing line. This was followed by a year of learning to swim from scratch to attempt a triathlon.

My wife did not like it when she could feel my ribs, but to me it was yet another extension of my new success. Then, someone took a photo of me, and in it I looked like a gaunt old man. This was not the kind of person I had wanted to become, and definitely not the reason I started my new lifestyle. I didn't like it at all. As I was training for an event, I maintained the level of exercise, and slightly increased my food intake to take account of my increased level of activity. A new kind of hunger was added to the distinctions, which actually wasn't a hunger at all: 'I am not hungry, but am eating to sustain an intense exercise session later today'. This was an interesting and amusing reversal, as I was starting to eat more in order to support my increased level of activity. Even at this point, it was clear that when this phase of highly increased activity ever reduced to normal, as it eventually did, I would need to ratchet down to adjust to the new balance.

Eventually, this phase of chasing the very limits of what I could do abated, and changed into something a lot easier to live with. The turning point was my second half-marathon, which I had wanted to complete in less than two hours. This is not fast by any runner's standard, but for me it was something I wanted to achieve, and had worked for three years to do. When I had finally got that, a part of me breathed a sigh of pleasure and satisfaction, and returned to normal. Every now and then, I would pick up a new type of exercise, and satisfied my need for change in this way, and also in other and different areas of my life.

It is clear that some people like changes every now and then, and are less good at doing maintenance in a way that things stay the same. It took me a long time to be content to really put my body in a maintenance phase.

I stayed in maintenance for a few years, and satisfied any need for change and achievement in other parts of my life. Once again, here I was almost exactly as I had intended to be right from the beginning, maintaining my success fairly easily and naturally. I chose to maintain a high daily level of exercise, not only to feel good, but to remove almost completely any constraint about how much I was eating. It was a great balance.

However, once again, another challenge was thrown my way when a ghost from the past came to visit. For ten years, I had been maintaining a low cholesterol level, low sugar level, low blood pressure, a healthy weight and all of the other criteria for a healthy heart. But before that, I had been inactive and obese for decades, and eating junk food throughout that period. During that time, this had caused the arteries in my heart to narrow to the point they were almost blocked. Such blockages are irreversible, even after ten years of healthy living.

I was doing a relatively light exercise routine in the gym, blacked out without any warning, and was taken to hospital. After some tests, they found the blockages in the arteries of my heart. I was told that if I had not adopted the lifestyle I had, I probably would not have survived many more years, or would have had a massive heart attack. As it was, there was minimal damage to my heart. Still, the blockage was bad enough to require triple bypass surgery, and this is not a pleasant experience at all.

Following the operation, I had an unprecedented opportunity to review and revisit the ten principles from scratch, and decided to adhere to them as part of the recovery process. It was very satisfying that most of it was already in place – the long-term perspective, the habits, the distinctions, the enjoyment of healthy food and being ready to embrace and enjoy a new identity as someone who has been through heart surgery and come out the other side. What was interesting was to pick up the eating and activity parts of the process. For a few days after the operation, I felt sick at the very thought of eating food. This was a totally new experience for me. At the beginning, I had one cereal biscuit for breakfast, which took me two hours to eat, a little nibble every five minutes. A total lack of hunger or desire to eat could be seen as a bad experience. And yet, what a fascinating resource this could be to draw on if I ever needed it, and of course it gave me the wisdom to help understand and sympathise with people who live their lives in this way. During the recovery period I was not able to do much exercise, and my food intake needed to be lower than it had been before the hospital stay. Somehow my body knew it and even when my appetite returned, seemed to compensate for it without much extra control or effort on my part. I put this down to the result of the mental investment I had made for the first year or two of my journey.

From an activity point of view, I started again from absolute scratch. For the first few days, just sitting on the bed made me feel dizzy, and standing up was almost too much to bear. I needed help to take my first few steps, but once I did, my recovery accelerated, and with the foundation of the fitness level I had reached before that point, slowly increased my ability every day. I was ready to take myself just outside my comfort zone, but not so far as to endanger my recovery. It was an interesting experience to rehabilitate, and revisit my original journey starting again from the absolute beginning, pretty much as described in the previous chapter. Doing it a second time round will help me become more effective and able if I want to help others start their own journey from scratch. At the time of writing, the process of reaching and maybe even exceeding my former level of fitness while adhering to the ten principles is still ongoing.

This part of the story emphasises the wisdom of adopting a programme such as the one described in this book as a preventative step rather than waiting for the symptoms of either diabetes or heart problems to occur.

For me, the process of maintaining my success is always there, with new challenges coming not only from life itself, but also due to natural body changes as the years and decades pass. Some of these are outlined in the next sections.

Making the transition

As you get closer to your target, it is a good time to review how appropriate the target is. If you came a long way, you might have chosen a target weight that is around or a little above a BMI of 25. For some people, this is appropriate, especially if their blood sugar has become normal. For others, they may decide to slow down and be a little bit above the target if they feel comfortable in maintaining that for the long term. Others still might wish to take it a little further and go a little lower. It is important to set up a stopping point, as too low a weight can also be very unhealthy. If your BMI was in the thirties or higher, it is unlikely to be healthy for you to go anywhere near a BMI of 20.

Also, if you came a long way, the chances are that any weight loss naturally slowed down as you approached the target, as each step along the way reduces your calorie requirement and also reduces the amount of calories you use for any specific exercise. If this balances nicely, it will – increasingly slowly but surely – go towards your target, and you will pass smoothly into the maintenance phase. It is good this way, and certainly better than struggling hard to get there and then thinking 'Yay! I have finally done it. I can relax now.' If there is any element of this, the moment of success can be a dangerous and challenging time.

Another way of thinking about this is that if you were never on a diet, and if the activity you have been doing is part of a lifetime programme, then there is nothing to come off. You simply continue exactly what you had been doing until now. You have made long-term changes, and now maintaining it is a lot easier that you might have found when starting the programme. The rewards of choosing and setting up the habits that were right for you can now start to pay dividends.

However, it is by no means over. People change, situations change, and even you may change. Life can be full of challenges, and your success depends on how you respond to them. Remember, you have some mental tools and useful distinctions to help you along the way, and hopefully still maintain a strong enough 'why' for how you decided to start in the first place, to keep you on track.

Be on guard

Even if you are now paddling downstream, and finding it easy and natural to maintain your success, there are some things to be on guard for.

The first is complacency: 'I am healthy now, and so can relax my choices on how I eat and drink'. That is true, as long as this is done either intermittently, or by invoking some other kind of balance. This kind of complacency is easy to adopt, and I must admit that I had periods of time where I got complacent. I stopped taking blood sugar measurements for a year, as after all, I was now an ex-diabetic. Luckily it remained low, but there was no guarantee that it would have done so.

Secondly is to watch out for new habits starting to slip in. Again, it is amazingly easy for these to creep in without really being noticed. I started to enjoy a glass of wine with a few evening meals, and this very slowly crept up to two glasses, and this slowly crept up to being every meal. By the time I recognised it for what it was, it was not so easy to change. In this instance, I chose to ratchet down, but still allow myself to enjoy it.

Thirdly, things can suddenly change around you, such as your workplace or indeed whether you work or not, your colleagues, where you live, family, injury or illness. Any of these can serve to throw you off course. Everyone will have different challenges, and all I can say here is that if you maintain a long-term view, and also use some of the mental tools you have built up, you stand a better chance of remaining resilient to any minor, or even major, upset life presents to you. This is also where remembering as powerfully as possible the reasons why you started this journey in the first place can be very helpful.

Another thing that can change, in either direction, is the balance of food intake and activity. If your exercise level goes down, you may need to make a corresponding adjustment to your eating choices, otherwise you might face a slow but steady weight gain. Or if you get athletic or competitive aspirations, you will need to increase it in a way that you can ratchet down as and when this extra activity burst returns to a normal level. I decided I wanted to eat a little more, and increased my level of exercise, partly as I got to enjoy being fit and becoming even fitter. This increase of activity gives me almost total freedom to eat what I want, knowing that if it should ever start to decrease I would need to readjust slightly.

Over the years

Even if you manage to maintain a balance for a few years, and weathered any storms that you might have encountered along the way, there are some natural biological changes that happen over the years.

One of the changes was mentioned in the previous chapters. Even if you maintain the same level of activity, your daily calorie requirement is likely to decrease by over 100 kcal every 10 years for a moderately active male, and a little lower for a moderately active female.

Another change, which is actually related, is that in general there is a decline in muscle mass with age. A good resistance exercise programme will help minimise the effects, but it is a trend.

Let us consider the possible plight of a person who is moderately active over 10-20 years, and actually maintains the same weight and activity level throughout that time. It is quite possible that they are slowly losing muscle and slowly increasing their fat storage without even knowing it. After a while the balance is tilted, and even though they are not doing anything different, start to put on weight for no apparent reason. This is often a puzzling and frustrating situation. If this is understood in advance, then a resistance programme, or a small ratcheting down of the calorie intake, can help pre-empt this happening.

Another change is that the body does not take up water as readily as it did, and with increasing years it is easy to take in less than is actually needed. Soon after I first started my programme, I built in the habit of drinking two glasses of water in the morning before breakfast, and embedded it in a little ritual that I do every day. Ten years later, I reviewed this, as I knew I was not drinking enough. I had lots of choices, and spreading more water throughout the day is naturally the best. In addition, I chose to adapt my ritual and drink four glasses of water before breakfast, just to be sure I started each day fully hydrated.

The body also does not take in some of the important nutrients like it used to. The concept of swapping bad food out for more wholesome unprocessed food can only result in increasing the nutrients the body needs so much. As the direction I was taking was to make my food intake increasingly healthy, for example eating more broccoli and oily fish, I did not choose to take any supplements. However, this is a choice people including myself may wish to review as the years pass by, especially as modern food production techniques often deplete the food of vital vitamins and minerals. If I were to begin taking supplements, the place I would start would be omega-3 fats, such as fish-based oils, to correct the effects of the imbalance between omega-3 and omega-6. However, my intake specifically includes oily fish at least two or three times a week, and I would always prefer to take my nutrients in from my food than from supplements if at all possible. Apart from that, I would not want to take any single vitamin or chemical in isolation. It is easy to think that one is short of iron, or calcium, or vitamin E, and start taking it in large quantities without medical supervision. With all the good intentions in the world, such action could cause a very unhealthy imbalance with very serious consequences. When and if the time comes, my preference would be a comprehensive and balanced multi-vitamin and mineral supplement, in keeping with the whole philosophy of the programme.

Final notes

When an aeroplane takes off and heads for a distant airport, it is actually flying off-course for much of the time, and throughout the journey the pilot needs to guide it back gently so that it arrives at the intended destination.

Similarly, the maintenance phase is not just a static phase, even if you are now paddling downstream. It needs checking out every now and then, reviewing and adapting your habits and choices to adapt to changes in your environment and your body.

There are no guarantees in life. Someone who has passed the diabetes threshold is likely to have stressed their insulin-producing cells, and some of them will certainly have got exhausted and stopped functioning. Those that have died are never replaced. With increasing age, there may be a further decrease in insulin-producing cells, either due to a genetic bias, previous stresses or simply by the aging process. So it is worth monitoring your fasting blood sugar at least one morning a week, and asking your doctor to take HbA1c readings at least annually to check for changes. And it could happen that your insulin production slowly deteriorates over the years to the point that medication might be needed to help keep your blood sugar as low as possible. Even if it does, you will know that you have done the best you can, not only to stave it off for as long as possible, but by keeping your insulin resistance low you can also ensure the effects of diabetes can be minimised for the rest of your life.

Looking back, the collapse that led to the diagnosis of diabetes was the best thing that could have happened to me. I changed my lifestyle, have more energy, more self-respect and more confidence than I ever had before. It probably even saved me from a fatal heart attack. I expect to live longer as a direct result, and I continue to build future plans. I hope that if you make a similar change, this kind of programme can add years to your life, and also life to your years.

Epilogue

As I look back over the years, it still almost surprises me that I was able to become slim and fit, and maintain it over the years. I still love food just as much as I used to, and often still think about the next meal.

However, something has definitely changed. My tastes are different, and while I still love to eat, I no longer enjoy the feeling of being overly full. I only eat small quantities of sweet food such as chocolate cake or Belgian chocolates, mainly because I am not really attracted to them any longer. This means that almost no self-control is needed, nor is there any kind of internal fight. It is really like paddling downstream.

New habits have been planted, and as they grew have replaced old ones. I still sometimes check them out in different ways. One example is leaving a little food on my plate every now and then, and checking out that I am still comfortable doing this.

I remain fit as I journey through my sixties, and am even planning a new career in helping people achieve similar results when I retire from my current job.

At my last annual diabetic check-up, the nurse was so pleased with my blood sugar results that she offered me a full diabetic test, consisting of the fasting blood sugar measurement and also the glucose intolerance test to check how my body copes with 75g of sugar. The results were what would be expected for a totally non-diabetic person, and even below the levels for prediabetes. I have now been discharged from the diabetic register, with full medical clearance that I truly am now an ex-diabetic.

What I have achieved is not unique. There are many stories from all over the world where people with far worse Type 2 diabetes than I had have totally reversed it. It is easy to say "Where there's a will, there's a way," but that spirit can require a lot of commitment and discipline. I suggest that "Where there's a way, there's a will" and hope that this book has shown that there can indeed be a way for you to succeed. I hope my story and methods, along with the knowledge that many other people have also totally succeeded, will help inspire and motivate people to confront and totally prevent or reverse Type 2 diabetes.

Nutritional values of some fruit and vegetables

Food	kcal	% protein	% fat	% carbs	% fibre	Glycaemic load
Cucumber	15	1	0	4	0	Very low
Celery	16	1	0	3	2	Very low
Tomato	18	1	0	4	1	Very low
Broccoli *(raw)*	28	3	0	5	0	Very low
Grapefruit	33	1	0	8	1	Very low
Raw carrots	23	1	0	10	3	Very low
Watermelon	30	1	0	6	0	Very low
Melon	35	1	0	9	1	Very low
Strawberries	32	1	0	8	2	Very low
Blackberry	43	1	0	10	5	Very low
Orange	47	1	0	12	2	Very low
Pineapple	50	1	0	13	1	Very low
Apple *(with skin)*	52	0	0	14	2	Very low
Blueberries	57	1	0	14	2	Very low
Kiwi fruit	61	1	1	15	3	Very low
Cherries	63	1	0	16	2	Very low
Broad beans	65	6	1	7	6	Very low
Mango	65	1	0	17	2	Very low
Grapes	69	1	0	18	1	Low
Sweet potato *(boiled)*	76	1	0	18	3	Low
Peas	81	5	0	14	5	Very low
Boiled potatoes *(in skin)*	87	2	0	20	2	Low
Baked potato *(in skin)*	93	2	0	21	2	Low
Corn *(on the cob)*	86	3	1	19	3	Low
Banana *(without skin)*	89	1	0	23	3	Low
Avocado	160	2	15	9	7	Very low
Figs *(raw)*	74	1	0	19	3	Low
Figs *(dried)*	249	3	1	64	10	Very high
Dried medjool dates	277	2	0	75	7	Very high
Raisins	299	3	0	79	4	Very high
Sunflower seeds *(dried)*	584	21	51	20	9	Very low
Flax seeds	534	18	42	29	27	Very low
Watermelon seeds *(dried)*	557	28	47	15	0	Very low
Almonds	581	22	51	20	10	Very low
Walnuts	654	15	65	14	3	Very low
Brazil nuts	656	14	66	12	8	Very low

Nutritional value of various foods

Food	kcal	% protein	% fat	% carbs	% fibre	Glycaemic load
Fresh Tuna - baked *(skipjack)*	184	30	8	0	0	Very low
Fresh Mackerel - baked	262	24	18	0	0	Very low
Tinned tuna *(in water)*	128	24	3	0	0	Very low
Sardines *(tinned in tomato sauce)*	186	21	10	1	0	Very low
Cod *(baked)*	105	23	1	0	0	Very low
Salmon *(farmed, baked)*	206	22	12	0	0	Very low
Salmon *(pink, baked)*	149	26	4	0	0	Very low
Halibut *(baked)*	140	27	3	0	0	Very low
Smoked Salmon	180	23	10	0	0	Very low
Oysters	72	12	2	1	0	Very low
Prawns, shrimps boiled	99	21	1	0	0	Very low
Chicken breast no skin, grilled	165	31	3.6	0	0	Very low
Chicken breast with skin, grilled	187	28	8.5	0	0	Very low
Rump steak	125	22	4.1	0	0	Very low
Sirloin steak	135	23.5	4.5	0	0	Very low
Minced beef *(typical)*	286	24	20	0	0	Very low
Roast pork	182	26	9	0	0	Very low
Roast chicken with skin	223	24	13	0	0	Very low
Roast chicken without skin	167	25	7	0	0	Very low
Roast turkey	170	29	5	0	0	Very low
Beef salami	261	13	22	2	0	Very low
Pork sausages *(unless low-fat)*	330	12	24	17	2	Low
Egg	155	13	11	1	0	Very low
White bread	266	8	3	51	2	Very high
Wholewheat bread	247	13	3	41	7	Medium
Chips *(French fries)*	319	4	17	38	4	Medium
Cheddar cheese	403	25	33	1	0	Very low
Potatoes *(baked)* with skin	93	3	0	21	2	Low
Potatoes *(hash brown)*	265	3	13	35	3	Medium
Baked beans from can	94	5	0	21	4	Low
Fast food Fried chicken**	279	17	20	10	0	Very low
Doughnut *(glazed)*	452	5	25	51	2	High
Quarter pound cheeseburger***	266	14	15	19	1	Low
Quarter pound burger	246	13	12	21	1	Low
Chocolate caramels	474	5	21	68	1	Very high
Dark chocolate *(70-85%)*	599	8	43	46	11	Medium

** Breast is lower calorie, lower fat. Wings are higher calorie, higher fat

*** A quarter pound cheeseburger is 200g. Double all quantities, and put GL to High

Calorie values of various drinks and dips

Drinks	kcal/100ml
Water	**0**
Tomato/vegetable juice	20
Stock cube as a drink	**30**
Tonic Water	33
Skimmed milk	**34**
Cider	35
Lager (5%)	**43**
Cola/Sugared soft drinks	45
Semi-skimmed milk	**48**
Pure apple/orange juice	45-50
Typical fruit smoothie	**55**
Whole milk	64
Wine	**64-72**
Brandy/cognac	175
Vodka/whisky/rum	**230**
Cream-based whisky	323
Crème de menthe	**420**

Food often eaten with drinks	kcal/100g
Japanese rice crackers	**370**
Salted roasted peanuts	585
Pork scratchings	**606**

Dips	kcal/100g
Cool Salsa	**60**
Tzaziki dip	115
Tomato ketchup	**103**
Guacamole	185
Soured cream and chive	**280**
Nacho cheese	350
Houmous	**325**
Taramasalata	515
Full Mayonnaise	**680**
Olive oil	880

Daily calorie requirement

The graphs for the Base Metabolic Rate come from a study by Benedict and Harris** in 1919, which although being slightly updated recently, seems to have stood the test of time. For those who prefer to calculate the numbers for themselves, this Appendix contains the explicit formula they published, which was used for the graphs in the main part of the book.

Here is the formula:

> If your height is **H** cm
> your weight is **W** kg
> your age is **A** years *(and is 16 or over)*

and if E is a factor expressing how active you are, where:

> **E=1.2**   if you sit around most of the day
> **E=1.375**   if you are lightly active
> **E=1.55**   if you are moderately active
> **E=1.725**   if you are heavily active
> **E=1.9**   if you are extremely active

then, if you are male, your daily Calorie requirement is around
{ 66.5 + (13.75 x W) + (5.00 x H) – (6.78 x A) } x E kcal

if you are female, it is around
{ 655.1 + (9.56 x W) + (1.85 x H) – (4.68 x A) } x E kcal

If you prefer to work in inches and pounds, the formulae are:

> If your height is **H** inches
> your weight is **W** pounds
> your age is **A** years *(and is 16 or over)*

then, if you are male, your daily Calorie requirement is around
{ 66.5 + (6.2 x W) + (12.7 x H) – (6.8 x A) } x E kcal

if you are female, it is around
{ 655.1 + (4.36 x W) + (4.57 x H) – (4.7 x A) } x E kcal

** *J. Arthur Harris and Francis G. Benedict. Proceedings of the National Academy of Sciences. Vol. 4, No. 12 (December 1918): 370–373.*

Calories used per hour for various activities

Activity	60 Kg	70 Kg	80 Kg	90 Kg	100 Kg	110 Kg	120 Kg
Walking, 2.0 mph, slow pace	151	176	201	226	251	276	301
Walking, 3.0 mph, moderate	211	246	281	316	351	386	421
Walking, 3.5 mph, fairly brisk pace	240	280	320	360	400	440	480
Walking, 4.0 mph, very brisk pace	301	351	401	451	502	552	602
Walking, 3.5 mph, uphill	360	420	480	540	600	660	721
Nordic walking (3.5 mph)	340	397	453	510	567	623	680
Running, 5 mph (12 min mile)	480	560	640	721	801	881	961
Running, 5.2 mph (11.5 min mile)	540	630	721	811	901	991	1081
Running, 6 mph (10 min mile)	600	701	801	901	1001	1101	1201
Running, 6.7 mph (9 min mile)	660	771	881	991	1101	1211	1321
Running, 7 mph (8.5 min mile)	691	806	921	1037	1152	1267	1382
Running, 7.5mph (8 min mile)	751	876	1001	1127	1252	1377	1502
Cycling, 10-12mph, light effort	360	420	480	540	600	660	721
Cycling, 12-14mph, moderate effort	480	560	640	721	801	881	961
Cycling, 14-16mph, vigorous effort	600	701	801	901	1001	1101	1201
Tennis, general	420	490	560	630	701	771	841
Swimming freestyle, moderate	480	560	640	721	801	881	961
Swimming, breaststroke, general	600	701	801	901	1001	1101	1201
Golf, carrying clubs	331	386	441	496	551	606	662
Golf, using power cart	211	246	281	316	351	386	421
Dancing, Zumba/aerobic	360	420	480	540	600	660	721
Dancing, ballroom, fast	331	386	441	496	551	606	662
Dancing, ballroom, slow	180	210	240	270	300	330	360
Dancing, general	271	316	361	406	451	496	541
Gardening, general	300	350	400	450	500	550	600
Typical aerobics class in gym	360	420	480	540	600	660	721
Table tennis, ping pong	240	280	320	360	400	440	480
Tai chi	240	280	320	360	400	440	480
Badminton, social, general	271	316	361	406	451	496	541
Squash	721	841	961	1081	1201	1321	1441
Playing piano, violin, trumpet	151	176	201	226	251	276	301

Acknowledgements

There are many people who have either knowingly or unknowingly contributed to the existence of this book.

Firstly special thanks to my family. My wife Linda supported me when I was first diagnosed with diabetes, and at all the stages along the way. That support has been there throughout the achievement phase when I was changing into something unrecognisable, right through the maintenance phase, through my recovery from heart bypass surgery, and also the writing of this book. My children, Isabel and Peter, not only lived through this, but accompanied me as constant exercise companions at different phases of the journey.

My doctor, Richard Ho-yen, gave me a push in the right direction when I needed it most, and many people who provided advice, guidance and encouragement along the way.

The book only started to take proper form under the influence of Mindy Gibbins-Klein. I am also grateful to Leo Groen for helping with the photographic artwork, and the group of friends and colleagues who reviewed the draft copy I sent and provided many helpful comments that have helped make this book what it is today. They are:

- **Dr J.G. Cooper,** Lead Clinician at the Department of Endocrinology and Diabetes at the University of Stavanger, Norway

- **Tom Godwin,** an Exercise, Health and Nutrition expert, who took me elegantly through my GP Referral training

- **Graham Bower,** who has bounced back from cancer and now runs marathons, and is also an NLP Master Practitioner

- **Monica Richardson,** who lost her left lower leg following cancer treatment, and is interested in seeing how this book can help her

- **Fred Marland,** who has on his own initiative already lost a lot of weight and brought his diabetes down to the point of no longer needing medication

- **Sue Marie,** friend, neighbour and avid nutritionist

- **Candy T,** a lady who would like to reverse her Type 2 diabetes

- **Roberta Montano, a** lady who would like to reverse her Type 2 diabetes.

About the author

For most of his life, Barry was totally obsessed with food and absolutely loathed exercise. Stuck with the belief that he would be obese for the rest of his life, he had totally given up and did not take care of his health in any way. However, at the age of 50 he was diagnosed with Type 2 diabetes. At that point he decided to take responsibility for dealing with it.

Barry is now slim, fit and living a much healthier lifestyle. His blood sugar has been at a very healthy level for over ten years without the use of medication, and as a result he has now been removed from the diabetic register.

Barry's approach was to change his thinking in a way that supports a long-term lifestyle change. He built some mental tools that underpin a successful weight loss and regain a healthy blood sugar level. The eating and activity changes followed naturally and easily. He has written this book to empower people to overcome obesity and diabetes, and to inspire people to take action to prevent them.

Testimonials

"Essential reading for overweight patients newly diagnosed as having Type 2 diabetes."

Dr J.G. Cooper
Lead Clinician at the Department of Endocrinology and Diabetes at the University of Stavanger, Norway

"Barry is a great role model for anyone looking to make permanent changes in their life to achieve a healthy, happy and sustainable way of living. Barry provides an accessible game plan for anyone concerned about their weight and blood sugar levels."

Graham Bower
Master NLP Practitioner and Exercise Fitness professional

"Barry has been through an amazing journey to combat a disease that was greatly affecting his life. This book shares both his journey but much more a deeper understanding of the physiology and psychology of diabetes. This with his personal experience makes this a very powerful book!"

Tom Godwin
Exercise, Health and Nutrition expert

CPSIA information can be obtained at www.ICGtesting.com
Printed in the USA
LVOW102006070413

327975LV00001B/13/P